A MIDSUMMER NIGHT'S DREAM

Teacher's Guide

Copyright © 1988 Harcourt Brace Jovanovich Canada Inc.
55 Horner Avenue, Toronto, Ontario
M8Z 4X6

Canadian Cataloguing in Publication Data

Roy, Ken.
  A midsummer night's dream. Teacher's guide

(HBJ Shakespeare)
Supplement to: Shakespeare, William, 1564-1616.
A midsummer night's dream.
Includes text of the play.
Bibliography: p. T30-T31
ISBN 0-7747-1289-9

1. Shakespeare, William, 1564-1616. A midsummer
night's dream.   I. Law, Harriet, 1931-
II. Shakespeare, William, 1564-1616. A midsummer
night's dream. III. Title.   IV. Series.

PR2827.R69 1988   822.3'3   C88-094128-6

Printed in Canada

88 89 90 91 92 5 4 3 2 1

HBJ SHAKESPEARE

A MIDSUMMER NIGHT'S DREAM

Teacher's Guide

Series Editor: Ken Roy
Contributing Author: Harriet Law
Notes for A Midsummer Night's Dream: Harriet Law

Harcourt Brace Jovanovich, Canada

Toronto   Orlando   San Diego   London   Sydney

Table of Contents

Shakespeare's England

Approaches to *HBJ Shakespeare's A Midsummer Night's Dream*

An Introduction to *HBJ Shakespeare*

PHILOSOPHY OF *HBJ SHAKESPEARE*

HBJ Shakespeare was developed in response to a growing need for an integrated language arts and student-centred approach to the study of Shakespeare. By providing a wide range of writing, speaking/listening, viewing, and independent project activities that allow for personal and creative response, this series assists students to recognize both the accessibility of Shakespeare's plays and the relevancy of the plays to their own experience, and gives them the opportunity to further explore Shakespeare in ways meaningful to them.

Students are encouraged to become familiar with and involved in the plays from the beginning of their reading by using these features common to all *HBJ Shakespeare* editions.

TEXT FEATURES

- Getting started – provides students with activities related to important themes in the play for discussion and/or written response.

- In this scene – gives students a brief scene description, allowing them to anticipate the issues they will encounter in the scene.

- For the next scene – offers students one or two predictive questions that draw upon their experience and provides them with a bridge to the next scene.

- Text notes – provide students with explanations for Shakespeare's text and help eliminate difficulties students may have with the language. These notes appear on pages that are facing the Shakespeare text and are aligned with the line(s) of text they explain.

- Illustrations – contribute detailed and historically accurate visual representations of characters and events. Illustrations appear at the beginning of each act and at the beginning of most scenes and help the students enter the world of the play.

- Activities – provide for personal writing, speaking, reading, viewing, and independent project responses from students at the end of scenes, following each act, and at the end of the play.

THE ACTIVITIES

The activities encourage students to further explore the issues they considered before and during their reading of the scenes. These interpretive and creative activities appear after all major scenes, after groupings of minor scenes, and at the end of acts. Activities that consider the whole text appear at the end of the play. Many of the activities are recommended for group work. (All the benefits of group work – such as accepting responsibility for learning, using expressive and receptive modes of communication in brainstorming, problem solving, and establishing a shared goal – can be derived as well from the study of Shakespeare as they can from any other areas of study.) In selecting and completing individual activities, students discover opportunities to:

- discuss the play, drawing upon their own experience;
- discuss and/or write about their feelings and responses to characters, situations, and concepts;
- make generalizations they can apply to new situations;
- complete independent learning projects;
- keep personal journals;
- create directors' logs;
- improvise, role play, or dramatize scene segments;
- make video recordings.

The activities at the end of acts and at the end of the play are generally intended to synthesize students' experiences of the scenes within the act. Many of these activities will require more time to complete than the end-of-scene activities.

Note: It is not expected that students should complete all activities at the end of a scene or complete activities for all scenes. Students and/or teachers should select activities appropriate to the students' interests and abilities.

HBJ Shakespeare allows students to join in the learning process by becoming actively involved in the play. We hope teachers and students will share in this dynamic experience of Shakespeare with both a feeling of comfort and a sense of confidence.

AN OVERVIEW OF THE TEACHER GUIDE

Section II of this guide offers strategies for presenting *HBJ Shakespeare* and for presenting a play in a condensed time period (approximately three to five weeks).

Section III offers historical and interpretive information about Shakespeare's England.

Section IV offers ideas for presenting *A Midsummer Night's Dream*

- an introduction to the play,
- the blending of different elements in the play,
- discussion about *A Midsummer Night's Dream* as Comedy,
- themes and topics for study.

Suggested Strategies for Presenting
HBJ Shakespeare

INTRODUCING AN HBJ SHAKESPEARE PLAY

If this is your students' first experience with Shakespeare, or their first experience with *HBJ Shakespeare*, you might wish to assist them in becoming comfortable with the text by allowing them time to discover and discuss the following features:

- the letter To the Reader that introduces students to the response-based approach they will find through the book and the Getting Started section that has them begin to consider important themes by drawing upon their own experience;
- the layout of Shakespeare text on right-hand pages and text explanatory notes on left-hand pages. Text notes are aligned as much as possible with the text they explain;
- Dramatis Personae – the list of characters in the play;
- visuals which appear at the beginning of each act and before most scenes;
- the "In this scene . . . " paragraphs which appear at the beginning of each act and scene and focus on important issues in the scene;
- the "For the next scene . . . " questions which appear on the page preceding each new scene and act so that students will draw upon their own experiences as they make the transition from one scene to another;
- activities which appear at the beginning of the play, at the end of most scenes, and at the end of the play. These activities have students explore many levels of thinking as they apply inferential, analytical, interpretive, and creative responses to the tasks they choose to complete individually and/or in group situations. The activities provide students with personal response-based opportunities to direct their own learning as they experience the play.

EXPERIENCING THE PLAY

You and your students might wish to discuss and record reasons for studying the play. After students have discussed and/or written their responses to the letter To the Reader and Getting Started questions, introduce the first scene by having students read "In this scene . . . " and read, view, or listen to the scene to get an overall impression of the plot and character development. Clarify any language or vocabulary difficulties students may have. Give students time to record individual responses to scenes and acts in their journals. Provide time for them to discover, react to, and record their individual responses to scenes and acts using the activities.

USING THE ACTIVITIES

The activities following scenes and acts have students use inferential, analytical, interpretive, and creative skills in their responses. Students should always be clear about the teacher's expectations for completing these tasks meaningfully. Note that because activities vary in scope and require varying lengths of time to complete, students will need assistance in selecting activities, and time provided for them to share or present their responses.

No one grouping of activities in an *HBJ Shakespeare* play will fit all class situations. It is extremely important, therefore, for the teacher to plan ahead, know the abilities and interests of the class, and have clearly stated objectives for the presentation of the scenes, acts, and activities to be undertaken.

Because many of the activities at the end of acts require more than the assignment portion of class time to complete, students should have the opportunity to work on them as the class study of the scenes progresses.

Care should be taken not to overload students with activity tasks. It is important to remember that although some students have developed skills in directing their own learning and are able to select and complete activities, others will need practice and support in developing these skills.

An overview of activities found in *HBJ Shakespeare* and strategies for facilitating student response to them follows.

Writing Activities
The writing activities present opportunities for students to write in a variety of modes and genres, for different purposes, and to different

audiences. These activities include writing items such as news articles, press releases, psychological reports, interviews, letters, journals, and editorials. To integrate a full writing program (including pre-writing, revising, and publishing activities) with the study of Shakespeare in a limited amount of time, you might choose a sequence of procedures such as the following:

Pre-writing
Pre-writing is often an on-going activity in which the student rehearses ideas for possible inclusion in writing assignments. The product of pre-writing could be a journal entry or notes made to prepare for a particular type of writing.

Students reading *Hamlet* might, for example, write a news report issued by the Palace Corps about Claudius's decision to send Hamlet to England. As a pre-writing activity they may wish to make notes about structures and styles of news reporting they observed when comparing the same news event written in several different newspapers.

Revising
Revising can occur at any time during the writing process. If students wish to have peer feedback before revising writing assignments, they could arrange peer group conferences. As a student reads his/her writing in progress, and points out a difficulty, other members of the group could offer ideas that may have worked for them in resolving a similar problem.

Publishing
Before students publish their written material, they may wish to apply a checklist including items such as points of grammar, punctuation, and syntax to their work. Students could publish a casebook or newspaper about the play, containing their writings during/at the end of the study of the play. They may prefer to put their news reports on the bulletin board following the revision stage.

Journal Activities
Students may wish to keep journals – a personal record of responses to issues in the text. Sometimes, these entries will be private reflections. Many entries, however, will be ones that students would enjoy sharing with a peer, in a group, with the teacher, or with the whole class. Teachers lend authenticity and demonstrate a commitment to writing by using the class writing time to create their own journal writing entries as writing models. These entries should also be shared.

The following is an extension of a journal activity. It is from the Act 1 "Consider the Whole Act" Activities for *Julius Caesar*.

Read through all of the journal entries you have made so far. Draw up a summary entry for Act 1. Use the following questions to help you:

- What have I discovered about the life and conditions of Rome in 44 B.C.?

- What have I learned about _____ ? (Fill in the name of several major characters.)

- What are some particularly interesting things about Scene 1, Scene 2, and Scene 3 in terms of the way they are presented to the audience?

Independent Learning Project Activities

Independent learning project activities provide students with the opportunity to direct their own learning as they explore new areas of study or develop skills to complete tasks they set for themselves. Many students show considerable aptitude for completing independent research and learning assignments while others may need practice and support in developing the necessary skills for acquiring knowledge independently. The independent learning project activities in *HBJ Shakespeare* are recognizable by their recommendations that students: 1) discuss the activity with the teacher and 2) keep their notes and rough drafts for the activity in a separate folder.

The following is an example of an independent activity. It is from the Act 1, Scene 1 Activities for *Romeo and Juliet*.

There are references to the mythological god and goddess Cupid and Diana in this scene. Find out as much as you can about each of these characters. What significance do they have for Romeo in this scene? Why have mythological characters such as Cupid and Diana remained so popular to readers, viewers, and writers, to the present day?

As you do research, discuss your work with the teacher to make sure you are on the right track. Keep all your notes and rough drafts in a folder.

Present a summary of your findings in an essay, a chart, or an audio-visual form at the end of the time specified for this independent activity.

The completed assignments may be presented to the teacher/class independently or in a group presentation such as a debate, a seminar, or a video presentation.

Scene Rehearsal Activities

These activities allow students to develop their dramatic perceptions of the play as they consider motivations for speeches and ways of choreographing actions, and requirements for settings and props.

When students consider the physical dimensions of an action, they often find that the dramatic content becomes clearer in their minds. For example, students often have difficulty following the sequential movement and seating arrangements in the banquet scene in *Macbeth*; but when they choreograph the scene, they gain a clearer sense of what happens and are better able to understand the cause of Macbeth's hallucinations. Likewise, when students act out the confused activity of the characters around the bushes in Act 3, Scene 1, of *A Midsummer Night's Dream*, they better understand the significance of the Duke's speech about imagination in Act 5, Scene 1.

Students could rehearse scene segments in small groups. While students are acting, you could move from group to group observing and highlighting problems they are experiencing rather than offering solutions. When students raise questions about their problems in interpreting lines dramatically, you could ask, "Why is that a problem for you?" You might ask questions such as "Would the character be standing or sitting when he/she says the lines?" "Why do you think so?" Then look for a group that has prepared an interesting interpretation of a scene segment and have them present it to the class.

Director's Log Activities

A director's log is a recording, either in note form or tape, of the ideas the group's scene-rehearsal leader wishes to keep for reference.

After a group rehearsing a scene segment chooses its director, he/she becomes responsible for conducting the group through problems it may have interpreting scene speeches and actions.

The director's log is the official record of decisions the group has reached with regard to the interpretations and the staging of the scene segment. It might include information such as

- how the group will create the scene segment,
- how the group will choreograph the action,
- where the group will place the action,
- what predominant mood the group will create for the action.

The log might also include the group's differences of opinion related to speeches, actions, and staging.

The log could record, as well, events that precede and follow the scene segment to give it context.

Directors who tape discussion related to scene-segment interpretations often find that their group gains helpful insights to the dynamics of idea-sharing by listening to the taped discussions.

The director's log activity is a useful strategy for having students combine some or all of the following skills: speaking, listening, writing, and problem-solving.

Improvisation Activities

Students often like to speculate about different characters' behaviour. By improvising, students often understand the behaviour of these characters better. It is easier for students to improvise a scene segment than it is for them to write a summary of the scene. When students improvise, they gain a sense of the character's motivation. Directors often use improvisation as a way of warming up actors for their roles. In improvisation activities, students use their imagination and their personal experiences to transform characters' speeches and so enlarge the life of the characters in their minds.

Listening Activities

Recordings
Recordings of selected scenes or specific speeches can be used to spark discussion about characters' motives and feelings.

Music
Students might enjoy choosing and taping music they feel would appropriately accompany a particular scene. A student (or group) preparing a reading of the scene could choose the music; or you could have one student (or group) prepare a reading while another prepares the "theme" music.

Viewing Activities

Film
To provide students with a sense of the whole play, you might set aside two or three periods for this viewing activity. Watching a film of the play before class study allows students to:

- acquire a sense of the plot, character relations, and shape of the play in one experience;
- appreciate the historical aspect of the play by seeing the costumes;

- gain a sense of the setting;
- become familiar with the language; and
- see the integration of language with character and actions.

Make a Video

This activity is time-consuming and requires careful planning and close monitoring. The time needed, from script to show-time, is approximately three weeks. Even the camera-shy student can become involved in the activity in some capacity. This activity stresses process as much as product and while it is a video activity, it is also a writing-process activity: it teaches concepts about narrative construction, characterization, setting, theme, and symbols, point of view; and the importance of proofreading, editing, and revising. Perhaps most important, it teaches co-operation and team work.

Although students are eager to grab a camera and begin shooting at the mere mention of the word "video," the camera shoot should always be preceded by a written or sketched series of visuals, or a "shot" list.

WHAT TO SHOOT

Establish time limits. Teachers and students should be aware that it can take from three to five classroom hours to shoot about ten minutes of finished video material. It is very important to select segments from the text that are not too long or complicated, that don't involve too many characters, that are neither too static nor too frenetic, and that are not dialogue-dominated. Have students shoot a sequence that does not go beyond fifteen minutes finished viewing time because it is simply too difficult to sustain evenness of quality in a longer shoot. Once students have decided on three or four possible scene segments, through rehearsed readings, have them test the segments.

CREATE A SHOOTING SCRIPT

This activity is the most important. It requires students to break down the text into "shooting pieces" in which the audio and the visual must support each other. The visual must highlight and support the audio (text, music, sound effects). To prepare for this part of the activity, students could divide a page in half and label one side audio and the other side video. This page will act as their storyboard. *Note: a bad storyboard is a bad video.*

When they edit their shooting script, have students consider the following:

A. Video

- Is each shot completely described? Do the visuals follow logically?
- Do the visuals maintain unity of impression? Is there an indication of what shot to use?
- Is the angle of the shots clearly indicated and is the mood consistent?
- Is the lighting effective and logical?
- Are the directions to the camera director included for each shot?
- Are the shots requiring action carefully blocked and well-rehearsed?

B. Audio

- Does the audio script support and reinforce the video portion? Will the audio fit the time allowed in the visual shot?
- Is the dialogue clear and logical? Is the audio script clear and coherent?
- Does the audio script support and balance the visual script?
- Is the audio script free from embarrassing mechanical errors?

THE FINISHED PRODUCT

- Have the videos transferred to one tape for a class video day. The class could be arranged as if students were viewing an important film screening; members of the audience could prepare and present reviews.
- The videos could be presented to a school assembly.
- The videos could provide the basis for a workshop given by the producers to students from another class who would like to undertake a similar project.
- Students might give a brief oral presentation about the importance of the writing process to the visual media.
- Finally, students could write papers on the process and difficulties of scripting a scene segment for video.

Video activities can be either group or entire class endeavours, depending on the class size. All class members can be involved with some aspect of the project. The following are some suggestions:

- technical personnel — camera operators, sound consultants, set-up staff, director, lighting consultant, set designer, prop designer, music co-ordinators

- on-camera personnel – actors, narrators, commentators
- advertising personnel – poster designers, radio ad creators, publicity personnel

EVALUATION OF THE ACTIVITIES

Evaluation is an integral part of the teaching/learning process. Handled wisely and sensitively, it can enhance the learning process provided that *objectives are clear, those objectives are communicated to the students, and those objectives form the basis of the evaluation process.* If careful attention is given to developing effective techniques for evaluating the process and product of students' activity-based learning, the evaluation will foster student-teacher trust, aid in measuring student progress accurately, and facilitate the entire learning process.

In *HBJ Shakespeare*, students are asked to complete activities which require the use of a wide range of skills in areas such as listening, speaking, reading, writing, viewing, problem-solving, and performing. They are asked to participate in activities by using group interaction skills and independent learning skills.

In evaluating student performance, teachers could consider these criteria:

- student understanding of the task;
- student attitude toward the task;
- variety of approaches used by the student;
- acceptance of responsibility for the task.

In group activity evaluation, teachers could consider the following:

- student willingness to accept suggestions from others;
- student attitude in discussion groups;
  - how well the student encouraged others in the group;
  - how well the student responded to suggestions from the group;
  - how well the student shared leadership and responsibility with other members of the group.

This information will help the teacher to assist the students in developing sound work habits, study and research skills, and social-interaction skills.

Throughout the *HBJ Shakespeare* activities are recommendations for students to employ *peer evaluation* as well as *self-evaluation* strategies in their approach to their learning experience.

The following are some ideas to consider in evaluating the process and product of students' work.

Writing Activities

These activities, which likely form the bulk of the student product, can be evaluated in ways such as the following:

- by formal writing assignments in which checklists are presented as the evaluation criteria;
- by journal or private writing activities;
- by a variety of writing folder activities.

Writing is usually evaluated using broad headings such as content, organization, ideas, mechanics, style, diction, use of language conventions, and originality.

Speaking activities

Evaluation of speaking skills is best accomplished in small group learning situations, dramatic enactments, role-playing activities, group and/or partner discussions, debates, interviews, panel discussions, and choral reading tasks. Speaking skills could be evaluated using criteria such as, does the student contribute ideas freely? make responses respectfully? take turns willingly?

Listening activities

Evaluation of listening skills is best accomplished during a group activity. That way student performance can be assessed in a give-and-take situation involving peers in a dynamic shared-leadership, problem-solving activity. Listening activities can be evaluated best by teacher observation of group participation in problem-solving activities.

The following checklist could be applied to the listening process:

- does the student listen quietly and attentively?
- does the student offer comments such as, "I see what you mean"; "The way I see it is . . . "; "I think this will work because . . . "; "I don't think this will work because . . . "

Problem-solving activities

Problem solving underlies all learning and happens most effectively when teachers and students are equal partners in the process. In *HBJ Shakespeare*, teachers have many opportunities to observe students' problem-solving skills as they participate in role-playing, scene-rehearsing, and other drama activities, and as they complete independent learning projects and viewing activities.

The following checklist could be applied to the problem-solving process:

- does the student hypothesize, synthesize, make analogies, and recognize possibilities?
- when considering unfamiliar concepts, does the student refer to personal experience as a basis for exploring varieties of materials in order to move from the known to unknown?
- does the student discuss, read, make educated guesses, and predictions about abstract concepts?

Independent learning project activities

In keeping with the purpose and approach of this series, the independent learning projects should be evaluated both for *process* and *product*.

In evaluating any of the *HBJ Shakespeare* activities, it is important for teachers to remember that the purposes of the activities are both to allow students to become a dynamic part of their learning experience and to encourage them to reach beyond their present abilities and extend themselves further than a teacher might take them in a teacher-centred environment.

Presenting *HBJ Shakespeare* in a Condensed Time Period

Some teachers may need to present the Shakespeare play in a condensed time period (approximately three to five weeks). The following suggestions offer ways to present the play using the student-centred approach in this series.

SINGLE FOCUS APPROACH

The class could preview part or all of the play by viewing a film to establish a focus for experiencing the play, such as one of the following:

- a main theme,
- a main character,
- the plot-line itself.

Having chosen one of the above as their primary focus in reading the text, students could then select to complete the activities related to that focus.

Single character focus

Shakespeare characters who are vital and inherent parts of the play experience and whose behaviour profoundly affects the plot development are appropriate choices for understanding and responding to the whole play through the single character focus.

In *Julius Caesar*, for example, it is Brutus (whom we first encounter in Act 1, Scene 2), whose behaviour most significantly brings the plot to its climax and denouement. The main themes of the play are revealed in his decisions and actions. Through Brutus, the personal and political conflicts of the play are resolved. Brutus, then, is a vital character in this play.

After choosing Brutus as their single character focus for *Julius Caesar*, students could direct their attention to parts of important scenes that include Brutus. Scenes such as the ones in the first two acts that introduce students to Brutus's strengths and weaknesses, and to the important decisions he makes; to the assassination scene;

the funeral scene; the final farewell between Brutus and Cassius; and Brutus's death might be considered. Students could then complete activities which focus on Brutus to further explore the language of the play, the relationships between Brutus and others, and his character.

In using the single character focus, students have an opportunity to observe and respond to the play in depth within the condensed time allotment.

STORY-TELLING AND/OR VIDEO APPROACH

A detailed study of each scene is not necessary for providing a complete learning experience of the play. It is quite possible for students to experience parts of a play without reading the script itself. Students often respond enthusiastically to the integrity and vibrancy of the dramatic experience when the play is brought to life by a story-telling or video presentation.

Similarly, students can fully appreciate the drama of the play when they see it on video. Students who are encouraged to respond critically to the choices made by actors, directors, and designers as they watch Shakespeare being performed, are likely to become enthusiastic and discriminating theatre-goers and media-viewers.

KEY SCENES APPROACH

After you and your students have previewed the play to decide what aspect (characters, theme, plot-line) is of most interest, you might designate segments of the play for attention. Below is a suggested procedure for approaching the five acts in a condensed time period.

One-third of the time for Act 1
Act 1 should be given careful attention so that characters and their motivations are clearly established, the issues and themes are made clear, and the plot is clarified. You may prefer to do this by playing a recording, by showing a video or movie version of the act, by using rehearsed readings, or by group discussions. Whatever method you choose, it should be one with which the students feel comfortable.

A focussed study of the first act of the play is important. It gives students the opportunity to identify characters and their motives, themes, and essential conflicts. Once they have familiarized themselves with the first act, students will feel more comfortable completing the activities throughout the rest of the play.

At the end of students' experience with Act 1, they may find that by completing activities from "Consider the Whole Act" they gain clearer impressions and understandings of the act's key issues.

One-third of the time for Acts 2 and 3
Select important plot development and/or character interaction scenes
to use as springboards for class discussion and involvement in end-
of-act/scene activities related to key issues. Since it is impossible
to have students explore all the play's conflicts and themes, assist
students in determining topics they may choose to develop in their
activity response.

Students could make journal entry responses to scenes from Acts
2 and 3 that are not focussed during class time.

One-third of the time for Acts 4 and 5
Focus on key scenes from Acts 4 and 5. The last scene of Act 5
should include discussion about the major conflicts, issues, and
themes in the play, recalling discussions about them in Act 1, so
that students experience a sense of completion.

A final writing, dramatic, or viewing activity could result from this
discussion. The group might wish to have a "video day" viewing of
the ending of a film or video version of the play. They could choose
to have a discussion about the play as tragedy (comedy, history)
or to present a dramatization of selected segments of student-pre-
pared scenes. Students might wish to debate major issues in the
play.

Summing up is important because it leaves the play complete in
students' minds and, although not all the issues will have been
covered, students will have achieved their own experience of
Shakespeare.

Shakespeare's England

HBJ Shakespeare encourages students to bring their experiences to the play. Like Shakespeare's audiences, students know about love, loyalty, taboos, leadership, revenge, identity, and ambition. As Shakespeare wrote in a time very distant from and different to our own, however, students will likely better appreciate the plays if they have some context for Shakespeare's world. You might wish to use the historical information that follows as your own resource and discuss these topics with students during their study of the play. A bibliography for Shakespeare's England appears on page T30.

WHO WAS WILLIAM SHAKESPEARE?

During Shakespeare's lifetime (1564–1616), England was ruled by Elizabeth I (1558–1603) and James I (1603–1625). Because Shakespeare was a commoner and only the nobility kept formal chronicles of themselves, we have only a few facts about his life. He was baptized on April 26, 1564, at Stratford-upon-Avon. Since it was customary to baptize on the third day, we can assume he was born on April 23. We know that he was the third of John Shakespeare's and Mary Arden's eight children and that his father was a glove-maker, a grain-dealer, and a man of some importance in the town who served as alderman and mayor.

Shakespeare attended a grammar school in Stratford-upon-Avon where the chief emphasis (as in all such schools) was on Latin. How long he remained there is not certain, but in 1583, at the age of eighteen, he married Anne Hathaway. Her home, in the adjacent village of Shottery, is now known as Anne Hathaway's cottage and has long been a main tourist attraction for Stratford visitors. The couple had three children: Susannah, born in 1583, and twins, Hamnet and Judith, born in 1585. Susannah married and had a child, Elizabeth, who also married, but she had no children. Hamnet died in 1596, at the age of eleven. Judith married, but her children did not live. In three short generations, the direct lineage of Shakespeare died out.

Sometime between 1585 and 1591, Shakespeare moved to London where we assume he spent most of his adult life. How he became an actor and a playwright we don't know, but we do know that he became one of the chief stockholders in the most important theatre company of the time (the Lord Chamberlain's Men) and a part owner of the Globe theatre. We also know that he became famous enough to draw a scathing insult from another playwright, an envious one perhaps, named Robert Greene, who called him "an upstart crow, beautified with our feathers."

When the Lord Chamberlain's Men were taken under the patronage of King James I, their name was changed to the King's Men. In this company were some of London's best actors, including Richard Burbage and Will Kempe. Shakespeare both wrote and acted for this company.

In London, Shakespeare made enough money to buy a coat of arms, giving himself the official status of "gentleman." For unknown reasons, he returned to Stratford-upon-Avon in 1612 to live in one of its finest houses, New Place. He lived there until he died, at age fifty-two, on the date of his birth.

The exact dates for Shakespeare's plays are not known. The following list gives a general frame of reference:

COMEDIES	TRAGEDIES	HISTORIES
1591		Henry VI, Part I
1592 The Comedy of Errors		Henry VI, Part II
1592 Two Gentlemen of Verona		Henry VI, Part III
1593 Love's Labour's Lost	Titus Andronicus	Richard III
1594		King John
1595 A Midsummer Night's Dream	Romeo and Juliet	Richard II
1596 The Merchant of Venice		
1596 Taming of the Shrew		
1597		Henry IV, Part I
1598 Much Ado About Nothing		Henry IV, Part II
1599 As You Like It	Julius Caesar	
1599 The Merry Wives of Windsor		Henry V
1601 Twelfth Night	Hamlet	
1602 Troilus and Cressida		
1602 All's Well That Ends Well		
1604 Measure for Measure	Othello	
1605	King Lear	
1606	Macbeth	
1607	Timon of Athens	
1607	Antony and Cleopatra	
1608 Pericles		
1609	Coriolanus	
1610 Cymbeline		
1611 The Winter's Tale		
1611 The Tempest		
1613		Henry VIII

WHAT WAS LONDON LIKE IN SHAKESPEARE'S TIME?

London in the 1590s was a bustling city of about 200,000 people. One of the first things that Shakespeare might have noticed was the great number of churches in the city. London was known as the city of churches.

The city was still walled as it had been for many years, but it was growing rapidly. People flocked to the city, causing a building boom of staggering proportions. The streets were narrow, cobble-stoned in places, but always dirty and crowded. Sanitation was unknown and plagues were common.

Shakespeare lived first in St. Helen's parish near Bishopgate Street and later near Cripplegate and across the river in Southwark. It was an exciting city for a young man from the country – full of strange sights and sounds. Since it was the age of exploration, there were many exotic sights such as clothing from the Arab countries, masks and charms from Africa, goods from China, and strange fruits and vegetables such as the tomato and the potato.

Since London was a port city, many languages were heard in the streets, such as French, Italian, Dutch, and Russian. A popular pastime was learning to speak these new languages, particularly French. Londoners received their education by reading books which spread in profusion with the advent of the printing press. It is estimated that there were over fifty printing presses in operation in London during this time. There were no public libraries or newspapers but "broadsides" (one page sheets printed on both sides) that reported news happenings in the community – especially murders, fires, deaths of important people, disasters of all kinds and, occasionally, bits of history – were sold for half a penny all over London on almost all street corners.

The streets were crammed with humanity. People begged for food and cried out for alms, shopkeepers called out to passersby to purchase their wares, balladeers sang on street corners, church bells called citizens to prayer, coaches clacked over the cobblestones, and water-bearers staggered under their loads. Londoners worked a twelve-hour day.

In addition to the noisy, sprawling markets, there were shops everywhere imaginable. Clothing was sold on London Bridge. Goldsmiths, grocers, fishmongers, and ironmongers also staked out areas to sell their wares. Even the wall around London itself gave way to shops.

Londoners loved entertainment and much of it was free. There were water games on the Thames, a small zoo in the Tower of London, cock-fights, bear-baitings, public executions, and, of course, plays, including those of Shakespeare himself, that covered just about any subject a Londoner might be interested in.

Despite the roughness of the period, it was not necessarily an unkind environment. Londoners gave generously to the poor, and London merchants experimented with various methods of finding work for the poor and the unemployed. And there was Queen Elizabeth, who made frequent appearances to the delight of the citizens.

Permanent theatres were rapidly replacing the old inn-yards as places of entertainment, and great actors were emerging to form acting troupes. New playwrights were springing up to supply the theatres with new plays. Shakespeare arrived in London when the theatres were thriving. It was a wonderful and glorious time in which to be alive and working in one of the most vibrant cities in the world.

WHAT WERE THE THEATRES FOR SHAKESPEARE'S PLAYS LIKE?

Inn-yards were favourite places for play performances in Elizabethan England because they provided a ready-made audience and because their long, narrow entrances and surrounding balconies served as makeshift theatres.

Stages were probably improvised from any available materials – some must have been quite precarious. The inn's stables and out-buildings likely would have served as change rooms, and stage properties would have been at a minimum. In the early years of these productions, performers took up a collection at the end of each play. In later years, the performers contracted with the yard-keeper to have him charge admission.

As plays grew in popularity, some actors considered having a permanent facility for their work. James Burbage, a popular actor admired by Shakespeare, built one of the first permanent theatres in 1576. To pacify the Puritans, who believed that plays were sinful, Burbage built his playhouse, called the Theatre, outside the city walls in Shoreditch. In 1577, another theatre, the Curtain, was also built in Shoreditch. The problem with Shoreditch, however, was that patrons had to walk over fields and swamps to get there. For this reason, theatre builders later chose Bankside, an area across the river from the still theatre-prohibiting city, in what is now called Southwark. In 1587 the Rose was built in Southwark, and in 1595, the Swan was erected there.

When Richard, son of James Burbage, ran into difficulties with his landlord over renewing the lease for the land on which his father's playhouse stood, he decided to move. He entered into an agreement with five of his fellow actors, one of them being Shakespeare, to build a new theatre called the Globe on Bankside in 1599. The Globe had an octagonal shape with a "thrust" stage projecting into the body of the theatre so that an audience surrounded the actors on three sides. There were three levels of balconies which enclosed the stage and an open pit in the middle that accommodated the poorer patrons. Drawings of the Globe indicate that only the balconies and some of the pit and stage were covered by a thatch roof. The rest of the theatre was exposed to the elements.

The Globe's stage was primitive by our standards. It had doors on both sides for entrances and exits and a recessed area which could serve as an inner stage. There was little room for storage or props and elaborate scenery. Above the stage recess was a balcony, and the floor had a trap door. The stage could be used, therefore, to represent heaven, earth, and hell – symbolism that would have been readily understood by an Elizabethan audience.

The Elizabethan stage provided an intimacy between actor and audience not possible in modern curtained theatres. This intimacy was sometimes hazardous for the actor if the audience were unhappy with the performance. (Some audiences, disappointed with the performances, became quite violent.) Theatrical innovations, such as the soliloquy and other devices to indicate the speedy passage of time typical of Elizabethan theatre, worked well on this simple stage.

The last big Elizabethan theatre, built in 1600, and called the Fortune, was square, unlike the O-shaped theatres that had been the norm. A stage similar to the Fortune's square stage was built in Stratford, Ontario, in the Festival Theatre, during the 1960s. Today we can see plays written by Shakespeare presented in much the same way as they had been presented for the audiences of his time.

As quickly as they sprang up, the Elizabethan theatres with their thrust stages died out, in part because they were licensed to make money for the owners, who traded on a popular interest of the time, much as rock concert promoters do today. Elizabethan theatres fulfilled a need, and when that need died, so did the theatres.

The Actors

Since all Elizabethan actors were male, all female roles were played by boys or men. It was not easy for the actors to appear convincing in female roles in broad daylight to their highly critical Elizabethan audiences. Actors were also required to perform very stylized and difficult dances that often needed both superior acrobatic skills and exceptional physical stamina. The dancing requirements were likely easy in comparison to the fight scene requirements, however. Actors were expected to fight as expert swordsmen. They needed technical skills and training as well as excellent physical conditioning to re-create duels and/or battle scenes without injuring themselves or their opponents. They had to perform actions such as running a sword through another actor's head or tearing out his entrails without impairing the opponent's usefulness for the next day's performance. Audiences of the day expected to see bloody deaths and mutilations in fight scenes. When bloodshed was involved, actors used sheep's blood because it had the right consistency for "running" well and it provided the audience with "real" blood. In stabbing scenes, actors wore concealed bladders of blood under their costumes. These bladders could be ruptured by retractable knife blades. When this action was performed correctly, the bladder worn by the character being stabbed was punctured, the blood spewed forth in profusion, and the audience cheered with glee. Performed badly, the actor being stabbed was injured (not an infrequent occurrence) and had to be carted off the stage, probably also to cheers from the audience. In this case another actor had to fill in. Since acting companies were small (perhaps twelve or fifteen men), actors were required to play many parts convincingly, often on short notice, and always to a demanding audience. Acting was a hazardous occupation in Elizabethan England!

The Audience
They were a rough group of people, usually consisting of working-men, trade apprentices from London, seamen on leave, and country visitors to the city in search of cheap entertainment. They were frequently noisy, boisterous, and given to violent outbursts of disapproval if their expectations were not met. They loved the sound effects, including cannons, drums, and chilling screams; the extravagant costumes; and the props, such as guillotines, fountains, and ladders. Most of these people stood on the ground, and so acquired their name, "groundlings." Dramatists like Shakespeare disliked these lower-class individuals and often portrayed them as humorously foolish and unsuccessful imitators of the educated people in their plays.

Surrounding the theatre were vendors, prostitutes, con-men, and pickpockets. Some patrons with money sat on benches in the balconies, while those who wanted to display their finery could rent stools on the stage. Members of the nobility may have attended the theatre for sheer adventure, but they usually arranged to have plays performed in their own homes.

The growing middle class attended a different type of theatre, which was indoors, had artificial lighting, special effects, a sophisticated satirical style, well-trained boy actors, and a higher entrance fee. Shakespeare's company of actors eventually purchased one of these "private" theatres (The Blackfriars), and produced many of his later plays there.

In an age in which the printing press widened literacy but could not possibly affect the lifestyle of the many illiterates, the theatre offered both a ready source of information and good entertainment.

WHAT WAS IT LIKE TO LIVE IN SHAKESPEARE'S TIME?

Shakespeare grew up in a chaotic period of history called the Renaissance. It was marked by both the vigour of powerful changes and the aftermath of drastic political upheavals. The decline of feudalism gave new importance to what would eventually become a rising middle class of merchants, shopkeepers, and professionals.

There was a sense of enthusiasm for expansion encouraged by Queen Elizabeth's emphasis on trade and travel to increase the nation's wealth. There were new ideas coming from students and teachers at the universities, and a sense of vitality in London that added to the energy and excitement.

During the Renaissance in England, guidance in spiritual matters was transferred from the Pope to the monarch, establishing the importance of individual conscience. Reformers began to look to education and the study of the classic works of Greece and Rome as alternatives to a single authority for matters of spiritual guidance.

On one hand, there were feelings of vitality, optimism, and national pride during the reign of Elizabeth. On the other hand, there was financial strain resulting from the prolonged trade wars with Spain. Toward the end of Elizabeth's reign there was also an increasing anxiety resulting from her having no heir apparent, a circumstance that would later plunge the nation into a disastrous civil war over the succession.

Shakespeare's life (1564–1616) straddled this period of hopeful change and the disillusionment that resulted from the corrupt reign of James I. Plays Shakespeare wrote during James I's reign include tragedies such as *Macbeth, Othello*, and *King Lear*.

WHAT WERE PEOPLE'S BELIEFS?

Not all people shared the same moral beliefs. Mercy, sin, pride, repentance, moderation, kingship, and God's power, however, were all central issues – important topics for sermons, for private conscience, and for literary exploration. The dramatic interest in Shakespeare's plays usually centres on the ways in which characters resolve spiritual, ethical, and political choices involving these issues. In both *Romeo and Juliet* and *The Merchant of Venice*, the issue of mercy is approached through a blending of Christian and classical ethics. In these and many other plays, Shakespeare portrayed the integration and balance of moral qualities as the basis of virtue and sound action.

"Providence," "fortune," and "chance" were important concepts to the Elizabethan people. Those who believed in Providence thought that God provided for and took care of those who trusted in Him. Protestants felt that Providence intervened directly when the winds changed in England's favour during the attempted invasion by the Spanish Armada. The evidence of providence was called fortune, a concept related to a person's fate. The image of fortune was often represented by a wheel upon which a person's career rose or fell.

Events manipulated by fortune were called "chance." Chance implies a sense of the randomness of life's incidents, which undermines any security we might have in predicting cause and effect. In *Hamlet*, we see Hamlet balance his desire for revenge with his concern that he may be misinterpreting providential "signs." In *Macbeth*, we see Macbeth realize that there are both good and evil implications in "chance": it may crown him King, but it may also expose his guilt when guardian angels "blow the horrid deed in every eye."

BIBLIOGRAPHY FOR SHAKESPEARE'S ENGLAND

The following references may be helpful to teachers and students if historical reading is desired.

Baugh, Albert C., Editor. *A Literary History of England*. Appleton-Century-Crofts, 1948

Bindoff, S.T. *Tudor England*. Penguin Books, 1969

Bowers, Fredson. *Elizabethan Revenge Tragedy*. Princeton University Press, 1966

Ferguson, Margaret F. *Rewriting the Renaissance*. University of Chicago Press, 1986

Frye, Roland Muskat. *Shakespeare and Christian Doctrine*. Princeton, University Press, 1963

Harrison, G.B. *Introducing Shakespeare*. Penguin Books, 1966

Holman, C. Hugh. *A Handbook to Literature*. Bobbs-Merrill Educational Publications, 1977

Joseph, B.L. *Shakespeare's Eden: The Commonwealth of England 1558–1629*, Blanford Press, 1971

Sandler, Robert, *Northrop Frye on Shakespeare.* Fitzhenry
and Whiteside, 1986

Tillyard, Eustace M. *The Elizabethan World Picture.* Random
House, 1959

Wilson, J. Dover. *Life in Shakespeare's England.* Cambridge
University Press, 1962.

Approaches to *HBJ Shakespeare's A Midsummer Night's Dream*

INTRODUCING THE PLAY

Attitudes toward *A Midsummer Night's Dream* have changed greatly over the years. Critics, from the Restoration period to current times have felt that the play is an enjoyable and light-hearted one, needing only music and dancing to make it a really good evening's entertainment. In essence they have felt that *A Midsummer Night's Dream* is a sort of Broadway musical. By the mid-twentieth century, however, critics became aware of the complex nature of the play, and began to recognize the similarities between it and Shakespeare's play, *The Tempest*. Today many critics regard *A Midsummer Night's Dream* as Shakespeare's first comedy masterpiece.

Students need some sort of framework or focus through which they may experience the play. One focus has been offered by Northrop Frye in his essay on *A Midsummer Night's Dream* in *Northrop Frye on Shakespeare*. In this essay, he says that the play employs parents as blocking agents to the happiness of young lovers. Shakespeare adds his own twist, says Frye, by putting older people such as Theseus, Hippolyta and Oberon and Titania at the centre of the action. In the forest which is a symbol for the subconscious, undertones of random desires and melting identities are played out with poetic, and sometimes menacing imagination. The lovers, old and young, are eventually released by the baying of Theseus' hounds to a world of harmony that is comical rather than celestial. The forest, romantic love, and the sounds of the baying hounds combine in ways reminiscent of ancient rituals to restore humanity to a stable centre.

THE BLENDING OF DIFFERENT ELEMENTS

In *A Midsummer Night's Dream*, there is a movement, as Frye has noted, from the opening scene which is hostile to the lovers, to the middle of the play where identities are exchanged, dissolved, and metamorphosized downward, to the play's final resolution where there is an emergence into light, love, and marriage.

Love with Marriage and Control with Ownership

The play begins with talk of one marriage about to take place, and ends with three marriages. We learn that Theseus and Hippolyta who were enemies and met in conflict, have fallen in love. But, in the midst of the marriage announcement, Egeus insists upon his right to punish his daughter Hermia, for refusing to marry Demetrius, the man Egeus has chosen for her. Egeus is interested only in his right to own and control. In a supposedly harmonious society we observe a system of justice without mercy. Hermia and the man she loves, Lysander, choose to risk their lives in their belief that life must have more options than the ones they have been given. As they flee the city, the play's movement toward the comic plot (the absurd vision of life) begins.

The theme of ownership and control in love darkens and shifts as the play action moves into the forest. Helena is jealous of her friend Hermia's happiness; Demetrius is furious at having his plan to marry Hermia thwarted. Both Helena and Demetrius pursue Hermia and Lysander into the dark forest.

The Forest and the Dream World

The forest, whether an actual physical locale or a symbol of the dreamworld (the subconscious) is a place fraught with dangers. The arguing that occurs between Helena and Demetrius attracts the attention of Oberon, the King of the Fairies, who is himself engaged in an intense power struggle with Titania over possession of a changeling. His seeming compassion for the four young lovers manages only to bind them more intricately into cruelties to each other. The magic powers he uses to revenge Titania, ensure that she will fall in love with something "vile". In her entranced state, she easily gives up the changeling to Oberon and so the forest world is returned to its original harmony. The young lovers too find themselves released from turmoil and chaos, and return to the city, armed with a new wisdom, ready to face growth and decisions.

Tradesmen Actors and Comic Vision

The third group of people in the forest are Peter Quince's actors including Bottom. The actors have come into the forest simply to find a quiet and private spot to rehearse their play for the wedding. They leave the forest profoundly affected by their experience while in "the green world." Bottom vows not to forget the "most rare vision" he has had—the experience of being loved by a fairy queen.

As Oberon and Titania renew their friendship and predict that three marriages will take place at the palace the next day, Theseus discovers the lovers at daybreak and announces the triple wedding. He sets aside the purposed hunting expedition, and overrules an ancient Athenian law so that the marriage between Hermia and Lysander can take place.

Bottom and friends also receive some sort of reward for their adventures. Their performance at the wedding represents their finest moment, and, as Snug believed, their fortunes have all been made. The would-be actors turn the tragedy of their play, *Pyramus and Thisby* into a comic-farce.

As the play draws to a close, Oberon makes certain that the comic vision has really taken hold here in Theseus' court. He enters the human world and blesses the marriages. Leaving nothing to chance, he also blesses the generations of children to come, hopefully in-suring that these children will not have to flee their homes to find solutions to their problems.

COMEDY IN *A MIDSUMMER NIGHT'S DREAM*

Just as Bottom, an amateur actor who reduces the theatre's fantasy to its most literal level, becomes the character who is changed into an ass by an act of pure imagination, so almost every event in *A Midsummer Night's Dream* is comically and fancifully reversed in this play. In reverse to usual patterns of romantic pursuit, Helena, an unrequited lover, warns Demetrious that if necessary she will change the "story" so that "Apollo flies and Daphne holds the chase." Queen Titania takes a lowly ass for her lover and treats him like a child. Lysander swears love to Hermia and then runs off with Helena.

The amateur actors also reverse situations, as they strive to make the fantasy of the theatre conform with reality. During rehearsal, Bottom calls for a calendar to assure the other actors that the play moon will literally shine the night of their performance. Bottom pro-vides the play with its most comically grotesque reversal: victimized by his own need to make the play literal, he literally becomes the ass.

At the end of the play, Theseus on the one hand dismisses works of fantasy as 'toy' works, and, on the other hand, recommends the power of the imagination to change reality so that the audience may enjoy a badly acted play. As the powerful ruler of Athens, he is fully aware that the disruptive powers of rhetoric and interpretive acts can change "a bush into a bear."

The uses of power, the concepts of self in friendship and love, and the attitudes towards theatre each becomes subject to comic reversals that provide the thematic conflicts in the play.

SELF-DEFEATING DESIRES

The lovers' suffering from comic reversals drives the play forward. The suffering seems to be occasioned by unrequited love and the threat of angry authority figures who can banish or send to their deaths unheeding children. In fact, the suffering occurs as a result of the lovers actions toward each other. Their actions give the play its comic darkness. As critics have noted: *the play is not a comedy about romance, but rather a play about the frightful implications of self-defeating passions.*

One of the most persistent, self-defeating passions in *A Midsummer Night's Dream*, according to critics, is the characters' narcissistic desire to be like each other, to be the same. Egeus asserts his patriarchal right to make Hermia in his own waxen image. Helena desires to rob popular Hermia of her sexual identity. Oberon wants to possess Titania's servant. And Bottom wants to simplify the complex relationship between disguise and reality by making them the same. He wants to play the lion so that he can explain to the audience that he is not a lion but "a man as other men."

To enter into such imitative desires, to want to see themselves everywhere and in everything, produces jealousies and conflicts—the opposite of what they desire. Hermia realizes this in her first love duet where she expresses her anguish over her father's insistence that she marry the man of his choice: "O hell! to choose love by another's eyes."

The forest, that seems to provide an escape from strife, instead becomes a place of comic darkness, where the characters play out in full their narcissistic obsessions. Here they change partners, converge on victims, and spy on each other's torment.

Presiding over the reversals and confusion inspired by self-deception, is the comic spirit Puck. He usurps his master Oberon's creative powers and leads the lovers into an ever tightening ring of substitutions when "two at once woo one." For the lovers, as the torment of confusion and hysteria increase, so does the sense of alienation from each other, and more importantly from self until Hermia cries out, "Am not I Hermia?"

Finally, Titania, victimized by her desire for Bottom transformed into an ass, is mercifully delivered from her adoration of him. She can now view him with disgust and loathing, and happily rejoin Oberon as his obedient Queen.

At last the Athenian lovers, exhausted by their passions, fall asleep and are delivered from their dreams by Oberon, Puck, and Theseus. The lovers are led back to the Athenian court, "where Jack shall have Jill / Nought shall go ill." United in marriage, they renew their love and regain traditional freedom, a familiar reconciliation in Shakespeare comedies.

And the dream? First it is rejected by Bottom. Then it is recalled with "parted eye" (or blurring) by the lovers. Next it is trivialized by Theseus as "toy" and dismissed as the type of "airy nothing" to which only a poet's imagination would give a "local habitation and a name." Hippolyta sees another significance, however. She sees bushes becoming bears as an ennobling process of the imagination that "transfigured" reality. She believes that because the lovers "witnessed" the same dream together, "something of great constancy" was created. Perhaps audiences witnessing this Dream comedy by Shakespeare might be inclined to agree.

Language of Comedy

The desire to be like others, and yet keep one's identity, that grips the characters with a self-defeating obsession, is a central theme expressed in the language of this play. Titania's love for a servant brings her to her love for the "shape" of an animal. Bottom's ignorant desire to make all fiction conform to reality makes him completely unaware of his transformation into a grotesquely real fiction. Helena's obsession with Hermia's powers to attract lovers brings about the convergence of two lovers and a friend-turned-enemy who "bait" her.

A variety of figures of speech express the double nature of the play's conflicts. These figures of speech work within a larger framework that parodies many contemporary traditions in theatre that Shakespeare delighted in satirizing.

Character self-deception is presented in several comic forms. Although the characters use metaphors, they themselves gain little insight from them. For example, Bottom at the moment of his metamorphosis employs a metaphor which shows only that he has intensified his assininity and ignorance.

Bottom: *Why do they run away? This is a knavery of them to make me afeard."* . . . *"I see their knavery. This to make an ass of me."*

Lacking insight into the nature of their self-deception, the characters become angry. Their feelings spill out into language of belligerence and war-like combat. The ruler Theseus, opens the play with a reminder that Hippolyta is his bride because, "I woo'd thee with my sword/And won thy love doing thee injuries." Egeus threatens to use his right to murder or imprison his daughter, and Theseus concurs that the law is on Egeus' side to "leave the figure or disfigure it . . ." The young lovers pick up this imagery, threatening lavish

T36

abuse of each other. Helena begs Demetrius to "use me . . . spurn me . . . strike me . . . as you use your dog" . . . "I do love you more."

Even Queen Titania's description of the the forest chaos becomes a series of quarrelsome phrases beginning with the "forgeries of jealousy", and ending with a "progeny of evil." Her subsequent bondage of Bottom follows with her command to her fairy servants to "tie up my love's tongue."

There is a constant comparison to animals as Helena implores Demetrious to treat her like a spaniel, as Puck boasts that it is easy to become an animal, and as Titania falls in love with one in her dream.

Characters make love equal with combat. Demetrious puns, "Where is Lysander and fair Hermia? The one I'll slay, the other slayeth me." Helena's, words, though in praise of Hermia, are fierce metaphors: she hopes to catch Hermia's sickness, catch her voice, catch her tongue, and catch her eyes.

The contradictions and reversals of behaviour are signalled by oxymorons, figures of speech that usually gives tragedy its poignancy. In this comedy, oxymorons add ingredients that are sometimes dark and sometimes farcical to the play's chaos. Quince's play is a "lamentable comedy" that is "merry and tragical," "tedious and brief." Oberon's forest, racked with lawlessness, is characterized by seasons that are in confusion. The forest becomes the setting for the play's central visual oxymoron, a queen in love with a donkey.

The use of puns increases the many confusions in the play. Metaphors that scatter the confusions and hostilities are the dream, the marriage, and the theatre. In each of these metaphors there is a union of dissimilarities: reality with fiction and lover with substitute lover. After witnessing the implications of their fantasies, the characters revitalize themselves by taking up their old traditions and expectations with fresh understanding.

THEMES AND TOPICS FOR STUDY

The following is a list of topics that students might wish to pursue in the course of their study of A Midsummer Night's Dream. Additional topics may be generated from class discussion and from teacher / student conferences.

Themes
1. Dreams are in accordance with the dreamers' wishes.
2. The purpose of a clown is to deflate popular myths.
3. The imaginary world and the real world are very different worlds.

4. The desire to imitate each other makes equality in friendship impossible.
5. Entertainment can be instructive.
6. Comedy, like Tragedy, examines human nature, but Comedy looks at the human condition more realistically.
7. Acting against established conventions brings predictable consequences.
8. The *forest* and the *dream* have the same function.
9. Magic is a symbol for the human imagination.

Topics
1. Power relationships
2. Midsummer madness
3. The moon's effect on people
4. Self-deception
5. Maturity and self control / youth and passion

A MIDSUMMER NIGHT'S DREAM

HBJ SHAKESPEARE

A MIDSUMMER NIGHT'S DREAM

edited by
Harriet Law

Harcourt Brace Jovanovich, Canada

Toronto Orlando San Diego London Sydney

HBJ Shakespeare: Series Editor, Ken Roy

Canadian Cataloguing in Publication Data

Shakespeare, William, 1564–1616
  A midsummer night's dream

(HBJ Shakespeare)
For use in high schools.
ISBN 0-7747-1267-8

I. Law, Harriet, 1931- . II. Title.
III. Series.

PR2827.A2L39 1988   822.3'3   C88-093587-1

88 89 90 91 92 5 4 3 2 1

Editorial Director: Murray Lamb
Senior Editor: Lydia Fletcher
Production Editor: Dick Hemingway
Designer: Michael van Elsen
Illustrators: Marika and Laszlo Gal
Cover Illustrators: Marika and Laszlo Gal
Typesetter: Q Composition
Printed in Canada by Friesen Printers

Acknowledgments

The editor and publisher acknowledge the consultants listed below for their contribution to the development of this program:

Michael Nowlan
Vice-Principal, Oromocto High School, Oromocto, New Brunswick

Marty Woollings
English Department Head, The London South Secondary School, London, Ontario

To the Reader

You may have heard something about *A Midsummer Night's Dream* or seen a production of it on a stage indoors or outside. Maybe you saw the movie of this story, or heard music from the recording written for the play. You may know that the story is, in part, about quarrelling lovers. Some directors have emphasized the comedy in the play; others have put more emphasis on the conflict. In this text, you have the opportunity to make up your own mind about the purpose and its effect on you as you read, discuss, rehearse, write about, and view the play's events.

Before each scene are one or two questions that have you explore ideas, themes, or personal experiences similar to the ones you will read about. You might want to discuss your responses in small groups or, perhaps, write them in a journal. Each scene is also followed by a set of activities related to the issues and problems that arise during the scene. You might want to pause after each scene or wait until you reach the end of the acts. Whichever you decide, you will see that many of those activities, just like the questions before each scene, call for group work and personal response.

If you would like to use this easy before-and-after framework for becoming involved in the action of the play, discuss with your classmates and your teacher how you might set up your journal responses. A date and a heading often will help you to focus and keep track of your own developing feelings.

Now that you have some idea how the play will be presented in the pages that follow, and about some ways in which you can experience the play, you are probably ready to start your first theme exploration. It is an overview of many of the themes you will meet in the play.

Getting Started

Midsummer evenings in Shakespeare's time were occasions for events such as outdoor games and special ceremonies where people wore costumes and masks. Sometimes these events were held in parks or forests much like summer events held in your own community. You probably are not as familiar with *A Midsummer Night's Dream* as you are with *Julius Caesar* or *Romeo and Juliet*. Its main characters are not historical figures like *Antony and Cleopatra* and *Julius Caesar*, nor are the characters famous in our culture, like *Romeo and Juliet*. So where do you begin work with this play? One approach is to brainstorm in groups any ideas or thoughts you have about the title. What comes to mind when you think of midsummer? of midsummer nights? of dreams? A second idea is to look at the characters listed on page 5 under *Dramatis Personae*. What expectations do you have about the play based on your reading of the cast of characters? After some discussion, your group could make a "prediction list," noting what you think the play will be about just from thoughts you've had about the title and characters.

Another approach is to answer some or all of the following questions. You might discuss these questions in your group, and record in your journal the responses you find interesting or thought-provoking. Because the questions explore some of the main ideas in *A Midsummer Night's Dream*, you could refer to these notes, altering or expanding them as you read the play.

1. Many people think that *A Midsummer Night's Dream* is a great fairy tale or fantasy. List the fairy tales or fantasies that you are familiar with. What characters, events, and settings are common to fantasies and/or fairy tales you know? In a few sentences, write your definition of a fairy tale. Write your definition of a fantasy. Decide which characteristics of a fantasy or fairy tale you expect to find in this play and include them with your notes.

2. Have you ever been in a relationship with someone and then, through a misunderstanding, found that relationship began to suffer? How did you feel while the relationship was suffering? Were you able to set things right? If so, how? How would you have liked to have improved the situation?

3. Should parents have absolute control over their children? When should parents start letting their children make their own decisions? Should parents ever be involved in deciding whom a son or daughter should marry?

4. Think of someone you know or have heard about who wishes he or she were someone else. Why do you think the person would prefer to be another individual?

5. How would you describe a jealous person? What makes people jealous? What effect does jealousy have on the person who is feeling that way?

6. Why do you think people challenge authority? Have you encountered rules or laws at your school or in your community that you feel are unreasonable or too rigid? Have you ever attempted to change them? If so, how have you felt during the experience?

7. Sometimes people are faced with having to make decisions that may drastically change their lives. How do you think people cope with making decisions that are this important?

8. How do you think someone who was lost at night in a dangerous environment might feel? Describe the feeling to your group.

9. Do you think having a vivid imagination is a positive or negative quality? Explain your answer.

10. Why are marriages usually cause for celebration? What wedding traditions are you familiar with? Discuss what you think brought about these traditions.

11. Sometimes people who think they understand an idea discover that an unexpected event changes their understanding. They now see the relationship or issue or belief from another point of view. What possible event might change the way you feel about a relationship? an issue? a point of view?

Many of the ideas that you have been discussing – such as friendship, love, jealousy, self confidence, imagination, tyranny and perception – are important *themes* in the play *A Midsummer Night's Dream*. The notes that you have recorded in your journal should help you understand the play as you experience it. Remember, too, that by sharing different opinions within your group, you will enjoy a richer understanding of the play's meanings.

Dramatis Personae
(Characters in the Play)

Theseus, Duke of Athens
Egeus, father to Hermia
Lysander
Demetrius } in love with Hermia
Philostrate, master of the revels to Theseus
Quince, a carpenter
Snug, a joiner
Bottom, a weaver
Flute, a bellows-maker
Snout, a tinker
Starveling, a tailor
Hippolyta, Queen of the Amazons, betrothed to Theseus
Hermia, daughter to Egeus, in love with Lysander
Helena, in love with Demetrius
Oberon, king of the fairies
Titania, queen of the fairies
Puck, or Robin Goodfellow
Peaseblossom
Cobweb
Moth } fairies
Mustardseed
Other fairies attending their king and queen
Attendants on Theseus and Hippolyta

Scene: Athens, and a wood near it

Act 1, Scene 1

In this scene . . .

The play begins with the Duke of Athens (whose name is Theseus) talking to the Queen of the Amazons, Hippolyta (Hip-pól-i-ta) about their upcoming marriage. Suddenly Egeus, a citizen of Athens, presents himself to Theseus. He demands that his daughter, Hermia, be put to death because she refuses to marry Demetrius, the man her father has selected for her. Hermia is in love with a man called Lysander and wants to marry him.

To complicate the issue, Hermia's best friend, Helena, is in love with Demetrius. Although Demetrius has flirted with Helena a few times, he wants nothing to do with her now.

The Duke tells Hermia she must obey her father. If she doesn't, she will either be put to death or be forced to become a nun. Hermia and Lysander refuse to be parted and come up with a secret plan . . .

1   *nuptial hour:* the time of the wedding ceremony

2   *Draws on apace:* is approaching quickly

3   *Another moon:* the new moon

4-6   *she lingers . . . revenue:* Theseus uses this comparison, called a simile, to describe his impatience to be married. He says that he feels the way a young man feels waiting to get an inheritance (money).

7   *steep themselves in night:* turn into night

9-10   *like to a silver bow New-bent in heaven:* a simile, referring to the crescent of the new moon in the sky

11   *solemnities:* wedding ceremonies

13   *Awake . . . mirth:* Let there be lots of fun and laughter

14-15   *Turn melancholy . . . pomp:* Sadness and gloom belong at funerals, not at our wedding

16-17   *woo'd . . . injuries:* Theseus had made war against the Amazons and had taken their queen, Hippolyta, captive. Here he is making a joke by calling their fighting their courting.

18-19   *in another key . . . revelling:* in a different style, with fun and happiness

20   *renowned:* famous

22   *vexation:* anger

Act 1, Scene 1

Athens. The palace of Theseus.

Enter Theseus, Hippolyta,
Philostrate, and Attendants.

Theseus: Now, fair Hippolyta, our nuptial hour
    Draws on apace; four happy days bring in
    Another moon: but, O, methinks, how slow
    This old moon wanes! she lingers my desires,
    Like to a step-dame or a dowager   5
    Long withering out a young man's revenue.
Hippolyta: Four days will quickly steep themselves in night:
    Four nights will quickly dream away the time;
    And then the moon, like to a silver bow
    New-bent in heaven, shall behold the night   10
    Of our solemnities.
Theseus: Go, Philostrate,
    Stir up the Athenian youth to merriments;
    Awake the pert and nimble spirit of mirth:
    Turn melancholy forth to funerals;
    The pale companion is not for our pomp.   15
                              [Exit Philostrate.]
    Hippolyta, I woo'd thee with my sword,
    And won thy love, doing thee injuries;
    But I will wed thee in another key,
    With pomp, with triumph and with revelling.

[Enter Egeus, Hermia, Lysander, and Demetrius.]

Egeus: Happy be Theseus, our renowned duke!   20
Theseus: Thanks, good Egeus: what's the news with thee?
Egeus: Full of vexation come I, with complaint
    Against my child, my daughter Hermia.
    Stand forth, Demetrius. My noble lord,
    This man hath my consent to marry her.   25

27   *bewitch'd the bosom:* used magic to capture the heart

28   *given her rhymes:* spoken words of love

31   *feigning . . . love:* lying or pretending that you love her

32   *stolen . . . fantasy:* made her fall in love with you

33-34   *gawds, conceits, Knacks, trifles:* small gifts; *nosegays:* small bunches of flowers; *sweetmeats:* candies

34–35   *messengers . . . youth:* all of these gifts can easily persuade a young person

36   *filch'd:* stolen

39   *Be it so:* if

41   *I beg . . ._Athens:* I demand my rights within the laws of this city

45   *Immediately provided:* clearly stated

47   *To you . . . god:* a simile meaning that Hermia should respect and honour her father

48-51   *One that . . . disfigure it:* As your parent, your father is your creator and he has absolute power over you, even the right to put you to death.

54   *But in . . . voice:* in this case, without your father's approval

56-57   *I would . . . judgment look:* Hermia wishes her father could see Lysander as she does, but she is told to look at Lysander from her father's point of view.

59-60   *I know not . . . modesty:* I don't know how I have the nerve (or courage) to say this, or what you'll think of me

61   *in such a presence:* before you, the Duke

62   *beseech:* beg or plead with

Stand forth, Lysander: and, my gracious duke,
This man hath bewitch'd the bosom of my child:
Thou, thou, Lysander, thou hast given her rhymes
And interchanged love-tokens with my child:
Thou hast by moonlight at her window sung.   30
With feigning voice, verses of feigning love,
And stolen the impression of her fantasy
With bracelets of thy hair, rings, gawds, conceits,
Knacks, trifles, nosegays, sweetmeats, messengers
Of strong prevailment in unharden'd youth: 35
With cunning hast thou filch'd my daughter's heart,
Turn'd her obedience, which is due to me,
To stubborn harshness: and, my gracious duke,
Be it so she will not here before your grace
Consent to marry with Demetrius,   40
I beg the ancient privilege of Athens,
As she is mine, I may dispose of her:
Which shall be either to this gentleman
Or to her death, according to our law
Immediately provided in that case.   45
Theseus: What say you, Hermia? be advised, fair maid:
To you your father should be as a god;
One that composed your beauties, yea, and one
To whom you are but as a form in wax
By him imprinted and within his power   50
To leave the figure or disfigure it.
Demetrius is a worthy gentleman.
Hermia: So is Lysander.
Theseus: In himself he is;
But in this kind, wanting your father's voice,
The other must be held the worthier.   55
Hermia: I would my father look'd but with my eyes.
Theseus: Rather your eyes must with his judgment look.
Hermia: I do entreat your grace to pardon me.
I know not by what power I am made bold,
Nor how it may concern my modesty,   60
In such a presence here to plead my thoughts;
But I beseech your Grace that I may know
The worst that may befall me in this case,
If I refuse to wed Demetrius.

65   *abjure:* give up

67   *question your desires:* make sure you know what you want

68   *know of your youth:* remember how young you are; *examine well your blood:* take a good look at your desires

70   *endure the livery of a nun:* tolerate becoming a nun (livery refers to the nun's habit, or clothing)

71   *For aye . . . mew'd:* forever to live confined in the nunnery or convent

72   *To live . . . life:* a reference to the vows of chastity taken by nuns

73   *Chanting . . . moon:* Shakespeare is referring to a time when many of the women who took vows of chastity were not Christian nuns but worshippers of the moon goddess Diana. Theseus calls Diana cold because she is a virgin, and fruitless because she has no children.

74-78   *Thrice-blessed . . . blessedness:* Women taking vows of chastity are blessed in heaven, but many other women are happier marrying and having children than remaining virgins.

80   *my virgin patent:* my virginity, or my right to remain a virgin

81   *unwished yoke:* unwanted domination

82   *consents not to give sovereignty:* will not obey

84   *sealing-day:* wedding day

89   *to protest:* to vow

90   *austerity:* severe strictness

92   *crazed title:* faulty claim for possession

98   *estate unto:* settle upon, or leave to

99-100 *well deriv'd . . . possess'd:* as well born and as rich

101-102 *My fortunes . . . vantage:* my prospects for the future are the same as Demetrius', and maybe even better

Theseus: Either to die the death, or to abjure   65
  For ever the society of men.
  Therefore, fair Hermia, question your desires;
  Know of your youth, examine well your blood,
  Whether, if you yield not to your father's choice,
  You can endure the livery of a nun,   70
  For aye to be in shady cloister mew'd,
  To live a barren sister all your life,
  Chanting faint hymns to the cold fruitless moon.
  Thrice blessed they that master so their blood,
  To undergo such maiden pilgrimage;   75
  But earthlier happy is the rose distill'd,
  Than that which withering on the virgin thorn
  Grows, lives and dies in single blessedness.
Hermia: So will I grow, so live, so die, my lord,
  Ere I will yield my virgin patent up   80
  Unto his lordship, whose unwished yoke
  My soul consents not to give sovereignty.
Theseus: Take time to pause; and, by the next new moon—
  The sealing-day betwixt my love and me
  For everlasting bond of fellowship—   85
  Upon that day either prepare to die
  For disobedience to your father's will,
  Or else to wed Demetrius, as he would;
  Or on Diana's altar to protest
  For aye austerity and single life.   90
Demetrius: Relent, sweet Hermia: and, Lysander, yield
  Thy crazed title to my certain right.
Lysander: You have her father's love, Demetrius;
  Let me have Hermia's: do you marry him.
Egeus: Scornful Lysander! true, he hath my love,   95
  And what is mine my love shall render him.
  And she is mine, and all my right of her
  I do estate unto Demetrius.
Lysander: I am, my lord, as well derived as he,
  As well possess'd; my love is more than his;   100
  My fortunes every way as fairly rank'd,
  If not with vantage, as Demetrius';
  And, which is more than all these boasts can be,
  I am beloved of beauteous Hermia:

106   *avouch it to his head:* declare it to his face

110   *spotted and inconstant man:* inconsistent, untrustworthy, unfaithful

113-114 *But, being . . . lose it:* I had my own business to think about and forgot it

116   *private schooling:* private business

120   *Which by . . . extenuate:* Which we cannot change (i.e. for a lighter sentence)

130   *Belike:* very likely, perhaps

131   *Beteem them:* supply the tears

135   *different in blood:* a difference in class or rank

136   *O cross!:* a reference to the crucifixion of Christ, and a mild oath in those times; *too high . . . low:* how unfortunate to love someone who is in a lower class

137   *misgraffed . . . years:* mismatched in age

141   *sympathy in choice:* mutual love

142   *did lay seige to it:* put an end to it

Why should not I then prosecute my right? 105
Demetrius, I'll avouch it to his head,
Made love to Nedar's daughter, Helena,
And won her soul; and she, sweet lady, dotes,
Devoutly dotes, dotes in idolatry
Upon this spotted and inconstant man. 110
Theseus: I must confess that I have heard so much,
And with Demetrius thought to have spoke thereof;
But, being over-full of self-affairs,
My mind did lose it. But, Demetrius, come;
And come, Egeus; you shall go with me, 115
I have some private schooling for you both.
For you, fair Hermia, look you arm yourself
To fit your fancies to your father's will;
Or else the law of Athens yields you up—
Which by no means we may extenuate— 120
To death, or to a vow of single life.
Come, my Hippolyta: what cheer, my love?
Demetrius and Egeus, go along:
I must employ you in some business
Against our nuptial and confer with you 125
Of something nearly that concerns yourselves.
Egeus: With duty and desire we follow you.
[Exeunt all but Lysander and Hermia.]
Lysander: How now, my love! why is your cheek so pale?
How chance the roses there do fade so fast?
Hermia: Belike for want of rain, which I could well 130
Beteem them from the tempest of my eyes.
Lysander: Ay me! for aught that I could ever read,
Could ever hear by tale or history,
The course of true love never did run smooth;
But, either it was different in blood,— 135
Hermia: O cross! too high to be enthrall'd to low.
Lysander: Or else misgraffed in respect of years,—
Hermia: O spite! too old to be engaged to young.
Lysander: Or else it stood upon the choice of friends,—
Hermia: O hell! to choose love by another's eyes. 140
Lysander: Or, if there were a sympathy in choice,
War, death, or sickness did lay siege to it,
Making it momentary as a sound,

145   *collied:* dark (literally, blackened with coal)

146   *in a spleen:* quickly, angrily, (the spleen was thought to be the organ in the body that produced sudden and impulsive actions); *unfolds both heaven and earth:* the bright lightning illuminates the sky and the land

149   *come to confusion:* are ruined, come to an end

150   *If then . . . cross'd:* if lovers always have problems

151   *It stands . . . destiny:* that is just the normal way things are

152-155 *Then let us . . . followers:* then we should be patient with our problems and accept our problems as being as normal for lovers as tears and dreams are

156   *A good persuasion:* good advice

158   *of great revenue:* with a lot of money

160   *respects me:* treats me

167   *To do observance to a morn of May:* perform the ceremonies of May Day. The arrival of spring, May Day was celebrated with dances, games, and festivities for lovers.

169   *Cupid:* god of love

170   *By his best . . . head:* according to legend, Cupid's gold-tipped arrow produced love in the person struck

171   *By the . . . doves:* by the innocence of the bird of peace, the bird sacred to Venus, the goddess of love

172   *By that . . . loves:* This refers to the belt (called a girdle in those days) of Venus. It had the power of being able to join people together in love.

173-174 *And by that fire . . . seen:* Dido, the queen of Carthage, burned herself on a funeral pyre after Aeneas, her Trojan love, secretly deserted her and sailed away.

177   *thou hast appointed me:* you just told me about

180   *God speed:* roughly, "good to see you"; *whither away:* where are you going?

16

Swift as a shadow, short as any dream;
Brief as the lightning in the collied night,   145
That, in a spleen, unfolds both heaven and earth,
And ere a man hath power to say "Behold!"
The jaws of darkness do devour it up:
So quick bright things come to confusion.

Hermia: If then true lovers have been ever cross'd,   150
It stands as an edict in destiny:
Then let us teach our trial patience,
Because it is a customary cross,
As due to love as thoughts and dreams and sighs,
Wishes and tears, poor fancy's followers.   155

Lysander: A good persuasion: therefore, hear me, Hermia.
I have a widow aunt, a dowager
Of great revenue, and she hath no child:
From Athens is her house remote seven leagues;
And she respects me as her only son.   160
There, gentle Hermia, may I marry thee;
And to that place the sharp Athenian law
Cannot pursue us. If thou lovest me then,
Steal forth thy father's house to-morrow night;
And in the wood, a league without the town,   165
Where I did meet thee once with Helena,
To do observance to a morn of May,
There will I stay for thee.

Hermia: My good Lysander!
I swear to thee, by Cupid's strongest bow,
By his best arrow with the golden head,   170
By the simplicity of Venus' doves,
By that which knitteth souls and prospers loves,
And by that fire which burn'd the Carthage queen,
When the false Troyan under sail was seen,
By all the vows that ever men have broke,   175
In number more than ever women spoke,
In that same place thou hast appointed me,
To-morrow truly will I meet with thee.

Lysander: Keep promise, love. Look, here comes Helena.

[*Enter Helena.*]

Hermia: God speed fair Helena! whither away?   180

17

181   *fair:* beauty

183   *lode-stars:* those stars used by sailors to navigate by. In Shakespeare's time, these guide-stars were believed to have magnetic powers; *your tongue's sweet air:* your voice

184   *more tuneable:* more musical

186   *O, were favour so:* if beauty could be caught like sickness

190   *being bated:* excepted

191   *The rest . . . translated:* I'd give it all to you.

208   *to you . . . unfold:* we'll tell you our plan

209   *Phoebe:* another name for Diana, the goddess of the moon

209-210 *doth behold . . . glass:* when the moon is reflected in the water

211   *Decking . . . grass:* dew

212   *A time . . . conceal:* the time of night that is always best for lovers to flee

216   *Emptying . . . sweet:* talking our hearts out to each other

Helena: Call you me fair? that fair again unsay.
   Demetrius loves your fair: O happy fair!
   Your eyes are lode-stars; and your tongue's sweet air
   More tuneable than lark to shepherd's ear,
   When wheat is green, when hawthorn buds appear.   185
   Sickness is catching: O, were favour so,
   Yours would I catch, fair Hermia, ere I go;
   My ear should catch your voice, my eye your eye,
   My tongue should catch your tongue's sweet melody.
   Were the world mine, Demetrius being bated,   190
   The rest I'ld give to be to you translated.
   O, teach me how you look, and with what art
   You sway the motion of Demetrius' heart!
Hermia: I frown upon him, yet he loves me still.
Helena: O that your frowns would teach my smiles such
    skill!   195
Hermia: I give him curses, yet he gives me love.
Helena: O that my prayers could such affection move!
Hermia: The more I hate, the more he follows me.
Helena: The more I love, the more he hateth me.
Hermia: His folly, Helena, is no fault of mine.   200
Helena: None, but your beauty: would that fault were mine!
Hermia: Take comfort: he no more shall see my face;
   Lysander and myself will fly this place.
   Before the time I did Lysander see,
   Seem'd Athens as a paradise to me: 205
   O, then, what graces in my love do dwell,
   That he hath turn'd a heaven unto a hell!
Lysander: Helen, to you our minds we will unfold:
   To-morrow night, when Phoebe doth behold
   Her silver visage in the watery glass,   210
   Decking with liquid pearl the bladed grass,
   A time that lovers' flights doth still conceal,
   Through Athens' gates have we devised to steal.
Hermia: And in the wood, where often you and I
   Upon faint primrose-beds were wont to lie,   215
   Emptying our bosoms of their counsel sweet,
   There my Lysander and myself shall meet;
   And thence from Athens turn away our eyes,
   To seek new friends and stranger companies.

222-223 *we must . . . midnight:* we'd better not see each other till we meet tomorrow night

226 *How happy . . . be!* Some people are a lot happier than others!

230 *And as he errs:* he is making a mistake

232 *holding no quantity:* having little value

235 *And therefore . . . blind:* In paintings, Cupid is shown wearing a mask to indicate that love is not just based on how someone looks, but also on his or her personality. We have the expression "Love is blind."

236 *Nor hath . . . taste:* sometimes there is no reason for loving someone

237 *Wings . . . haste:* love can be sudden

238-239 *And therefore . . . beguiled:* like a child, love is spontaneous, or doesn't stop to think, and is often fooled. This speech, lines 234-239, refers to Demetrius being in love with Hermia, when Hermia does not love him back.

240-241 *As waggish . . . everywhere:* boastful boys tell lies when they are playing, and many people, playing at love, lie also

242 *eyne:* eyes, before Demetrius noticed Hermia

248 *intelligence:* piece of information

249 *a dear expense:* telling Demetrius about Hermia's plan may cost Helena her friendship with Hermia

251 *To have . . . again:* I will follow him (and be able to see him) as he goes into the woods after Hermia

Farewell, sweet playfellow: pray thou for us;　　　　220
And good luck grant thee thy Demetrius!
Keep word, Lysander: we must starve our sight
From lovers' food till morrow deep midnight.
Lysander: I will, my Hermia.　　　　　[*Exit Hermia.*]
　　　　　　　　Helena, adieu;
As you on him, Demetrius dote on you!　　　[*Exit.*] 225
Helena: How happy some o'er other some can be!
Through Athens I am thought as fair as she.
But what of that? Demetrius thinks not so;
He will not know what all but he do know:
And as he errs, doting on Hermia's eyes,　　　　230
So I, admiring of his qualities:
Things base and vile, holding no quantity,
Love can transpose to form and dignity:
Love looks not with the eyes, but with the mind;
And therefore is wing'd Cupid painted blind:　　　235
Nor hath Love's mind of any judgment taste;
Wings and no eyes figure unheedy haste:
And therefore is Love said to be a child,
Because in choice he is so oft beguiled.
As waggish boys in game themselves forswear,　　240
So the boy Love is perjured everywhere:
For ere Demetrius look'd on Hermia's eyne,
He hail'd down oaths that he was only mine;
And when this hail some heat from Hermia felt,
So he dissolved, and showers of oaths did melt.　　245
I will go tell him of fair Hermia's flight:
Then to the wood will he to-morrow night
Pursue her; and for this intelligence
If I have thanks, it is a dear expense:
But herein mean I to enrich my pain,　　　　250
To have his sight thither and back again.　　　[*Exit.*]

Act 1, Scene 1: Activities

1. Hippolyta was already ruler and Queen of the Amazons when Theseus captured her in war. Look back at Theseus' speeches in this scene. What are some of the things he says to show the audience he is in command in Athens?

   If you, like Hippolyta, had a career before you married, what concerns might you have about your role in the marriage and your career after you got married?

   Write a diary entry about your concerns related to combining your career with a marriage.

2. Egeus accuses Lysander of bewitching his daughter Hermia. Why might Egeus think this way? What would you want to reply to Egeus?

   In your groups discuss some pieces of advice you could pass along to Egeus. Write one or two comments you would make in a book titled *Between Parent and Teenager*.

   If you were a guidance counsellor, how would you suggest Egeus and Hermia settle their problem? With two classmates, role-play a situation in which Egeus and Hermia receive counselling related to their problem.

3. Hermia says she doesn't know what gave her the courage to rebel against her father's wishes.

   What is your definition of courage? In groups talk about your ideas. Explain what you feel is "courageous behaviour" in women and men in your community today.

4. Helena hopes Demetrius will transfer his affections from Hermia to her, so she begs Hermia "teach me how you look" (line 192).

   In your opinion, is Hermia's advice helpful? What advice might you give Helena if you were Hermia? In your journal, write the suggestions you would make to Helena.

5. Could Helena's adoration of Hermia be a cover for deeper, less positive feelings? As Helena, write a brief note to Hermia asking for advice, but including hints of other feelings.

   Exchange your note with a writing partner. Read between the lines to find hidden feelings in the note you receive and write a response.

6. Have you ever been in a situation like Helena's (or known someone who was), in which you liked someone who didn't like you? Have you ever been in Demetrius' situation, knowing that someone liked you but wishing that person would leave you alone? Write one of the following:

   a) a letter to Helena in which you try to help her.
   b) a letter to Demetrius suggesting ways to discourage Helena's interest in him.

7. In your journal list the main characters introduced in this scene, and note your impressions of each one's personality. If you were in charge of casting for a movie, what actors or actresses would you choose to play these characters? What notes might you, as a director, make in your journal about the personality trait you wanted each member of the cast to emphasize?

For the next scene . . .

Many people enjoy performing for others. What do you think makes drama appealing to the performers? Would you like to be part of a group of professional or amateur performers? Why or why not?

Act 1, Scene 2

In this scene . . .

At the beginning of the play, the Duke announced that all of Athens would take part in his wedding celebrations. In this scene, a group of amateur actors meet to prepare the play they will present for the bride and groom at the wedding. Peter Quince, the director, assigns parts, and Nick Bottom, one of the actors, adds a suggestion for every direction that Quince gives. All the actors agree to begin rehearsing in the woods the next night.

Stage direction

The names of these characters reflect their occupations: Bottom, a weaver, is named after the object around which thread is wound; Quince is a carpenter whose name means a wedge-shaped piece of wood; Snug, also a carpenter, joins pieces of wood to make them fit snugly; Snout, a tinker, repairs kettle snouts or spouts; Flute is a bellows-mender. The word "flute" comes from the Latin word "blow." Bellows are used to start up a fire by blowing on hot coals; Starveling is a tailor, and the popular belief was that tailors were poor and thin.

2   *You were . . . man:* Call each man individually, by his name. Bottom says "generally" when he means "individually." Bottom often uses the word which is the opposite of the word he means.

3   *scrip:* script; the written list of actors

5   *interlude:* a brief play

8-9   *treats on:* is about

9-10   *grow to a point:* come to your conclusion

11   *marry:* swearing – an expression meaning literally, "By the Virgin Mary," in common usage at the time as a mild oath; *lamentable:* sad, mournful

15   *spread yourselves:* roughly means "Get ready"

20   *most gallant:* most gallantly, or most bravely

21   *ask some tears:* require that I cry

22   *let the audience . . . eyes:* the audience will cry with me

23   *condole in some measure:* grieve greatly

23-24 *To the rest:* name the other parts

24   *yet my . . . tyrant:* I would really like to act the part of the tyrant

25   *Ercles:* Hercules; *rarely:* very well

25-26 *to tear . . . split:* a popular expression at the time meaning to rant and rave with great commotion

27-34 *The raging rocks . . . Fates:* Bottom is reciting a poem to prove how well he could play a tyrant.

Scene 2

Athens. Quince's house.

Enter Quince, Snug, Bottom,
Flute, Snout, and Starveling.

Quince: Is all our company here?
Bottom: You were best to call them generally, man by man,
    according to the scrip.
Quince: Here is the scroll of every man's name, which is
    thought fit, through all Athens, to play in our interlude   5
    before the duke and the duchess, on his wedding-
    day at night.
Bottom: First, good Peter Quince, say what the play treats
    on, then read the names of the actors, and so grow
    to a point.   10
Quince: Marry, our play is, The most lamentable comedy,
    and most cruel death of Pyramus and Thisby.
Bottom: A very good piece of work, I assure you, and a
    merry. Now, good Peter Quince, call forth your actors
    by the scroll. Masters, spread yourselves.   15
Quince: Answer as I call you. Nick Bottom, the weaver.
Bottom: Ready. Name what part I am for, and proceed.
Quince: You, Nick Bottom, are set down for Pyramus.
Bottom: What is Pyramus? a lover, or a tyrant?
Quince: A lover, that kills himself most gallant for love.   20
Bottom: That will ask some tears in the true performing of
    it: if I do it, let the audience look to their eyes; I
    will move storms, I will condole in some measure. To
    the rest: yet my chief humour is for a tyrant: I could
    play Ercles rarely, or a part to tear a cat in, to make   25
    all split.

        The raging rocks
        And shivering shocks
        Shall break the locks
            Of prison gates;   30

31   *Phibbus' car:* the sun – the chariot of Phoebus, the sun-god

36   *vein:* style

40   *wandering knight:* a knight seeking adventure

44   *That's all one:* that doesn't matter

45   *as small as you will:* in as high-pitched a voice as you can (that is, to sound like a female)

46   *An:* if

60   *fitted:* cast

62   *slow of study:* not fast at learning my lines

63   *extempore:* without rehearsal, ad lib

And Phibbus' car
Shall shine from far
And make and mar
The foolish Fates.

This was lofty! Now name the rest of the players. This   35
is Ercles' vein, a tyrant's vein; a lover is more
condoling.

Quince: Francis Flute, the bellows-mender.

Flute: Here, Peter Quince.

Quince: Flute, you must take Thisby on you.

Flute: What is Thisby? a wandering knight?   40

Quince: It is the lady that Pyramus must love.

Flute: Nay, faith, let not me play a woman; I have a beard
coming.

Quince: That's all one: you shall play it in a mask, and you
may speak as small as you will.   45

Bottom: An I may hide my face, let me play Thisby too.
I'll speak in a monstrous little voice, "Thisne, Thisne";
"Ah Pyramus, my lover dear! thy Thisby dear, and
lady dear!"

Quince: No, no; you must play Pyramus: and, Flute, you   50
Thisby.

Bottom: Well, proceed.

Quince: Robin Starveling, the tailor.

Starveling: Here, Peter Quince.

Quince: Robin Starveling, you must play Thisby's mother.   55
Tom Snout, the tinker.

Snout: Here, Peter Quince.

Quince: You, Pyramus' father: myself, Thisby's father. Snug,
the joiner; you, the lion's part: and, I hope, here is a
play fitted.   60

Snug: Have you the lion's part written? pray you, if it be,
give it me, for I am slow of study.

Quince: You may do it extempore, for it is nothing but
roaring.

Bottom: Let me play the lion too: I will roar, that I will do   65
any man's heart good to hear me; I will roar, that I
will make the duke say, "Let him roar again, let him
roar again."

74   *no more discretion:* no other choice

75   *aggravate:* the word means to make bigger or to exaggerate, but Bottom uses it thinking it means to...

77   *an 'twere:* as if it were

79   *proper:* handsome

Peter Quince's notes
- on rehearsal
+ what has happened
√ things to work on

or p33 Act 1 NO 1.

85   *discharge:* perform

88-89   *Some of your . . . barefaced:* a sexual pun referring to the loss of hair from syphilis, which was called the French disease

91   *con:* know, memorize

94   *dogged with company:* bothered with people

95   *devices:* plans – that is, their play

95-96   *a bill of properties:* a list of props

99   *obscenely:* Bottom may connect this word with "seen" and mean "without being observed."

102   *hold . . . strings:* this expression is probably taken from archery. If an archer failed to show up at a tournament, his team-mates were allowed to cut the string on his bow. Here the line means, "Keep your promise and show up."

Quince: An you should do it too terribly, you would fright
the duchess and the ladies, that they would shriek: 70
and that were enough to hang us all.

All: That would hang us, every mother's son.

Bottom: I grant you, friends, if you should fright the ladies
out of their wits, they would have no more discretion
but to hang us: but I will aggravate my voice so that I   75
will roar you as gently as any sucking dove; I will roar
you an 'twere any nightingale.

Quince: You can play no part but Pyramus; for Pyramus is
a sweet-faced man; a proper man, as one shall see in
a summer's day; a most lovely gentleman-like man: 80
therefore you must needs play Pyramus.

Bottom: Well, I will undertake it. What beard were I best
to play it in?

Quince: Why, what you will.

Bottom: I will discharge it in either your straw-colour beard,   85
your orange-tawny beard, your purple-ingrain beard
or your French-crown-colour beard, your perfect yellow.

Quince: Some of your French crowns have no hair at all,
and then you will play barefaced. But, masters, here are
your parts: and I am to entreat you, request you and   90
desire you, to con them by to-morrow night; and meet
me in the palace wood, a mile without the town, by
moonlight; there will we rehearse, for if we meet in the
city, we shall be dogged with company, and our
devices known. In the meantime I will draw a bill of   95
properties, such as our play wants. I pray you, fail me
not.

Bottom: We will meet; and there we may rehearse most
obscenely and courageously. Take pains; be perfect:
adieu.   100

Quince: At the duke's oak we meet.

Bottom: Enough; hold or cut bow-strings.   [*Exeunt.*]

Act 1, Scene 2: Activities

1. Bottom often uses words incorrectly. An example of his incorrect useage occurs in line 2, when he says "to call them *generally* " when he means "to call them *individually*."

   In your group, prepare a Nick Bottom "Dictionary of Confusibles." Write out a list of the words he confuses and draw cartoons to illustrate them. You could add words that you confused when you were younger. Display your dictionary with illustrations for others to view.

2. Suppose you were the casting director looking for an actor to play the part of Bottom. Examine the ads appearing in the Help Wanted section of newspapers you know to observe the format used when advertising for help. Then write the ad you would place in a theatre magazine for an actor to take Bottom's role.

3. Bottom's imagination is straight forward. He knows only the following two types of male roles:
   a) the tragic grieving lover
   b) the raging tyrant.

   In your journal, write a detailed description of a popular actor or entertainer you know, who Bottom would think plays the role of one of these two male types. Describe another entertainment figure who often plays the kind of role Bottom might have difficulty imagining. Compare your descriptions of character roles with those written by a partner. Talk about the character roles you have described that Bottom has not recognized.

4. During Shakespeare's time, the actors frequently added 'slapstick' touches to the Player scenes. For example, in one production, the actor playing Bottom pretended that his sword got stuck as he tried to draw it from its sheath.

   What other slapstick "problems" do you predict could happen to Quince's players when they perform "Pyramus and Thisbe" as they try to manage their props, costumes, and the staging of the play?

In your group, suggest a few examples of slapstick situations where something goes wrong during the performance of the play. Perform one of the situations for another group.

Act 1: Consider the Whole Act

1. You are the director. Prepare the scene between Egeus, Theseus, Hermia, Lysander, and Demetrius (Scene 1, lines 20-127) for presentation. Consider the following:
   • What type of presentation you will give (modern English version, Shakespearean form, soap-opera style, pantomime).
   • What main ideas and feeling you want to communicate and how you will convey them.
   • Who you will choose for the various parts.
   • How you will show the relationships between the characters.
   Working with a group, direct the scene segment and present it to the class.

2. Choose one of the major characters introduced in Act 1 and record in your journal obvious images the character has used in his or her conversations up to this point. Note your observations about the character's personality based on the use of these images. As you continue through the play, you could add images the character uses at later points. At the end of the play, suggest major personality traits of the character from clues given by the images he or she used.

3. Many, many songs are written about love and the complications of love. If you had to select songs that would provide background music for a presentation of segments from Act 1, Scene 1, which songs would you choose? Would your choices be contemporary popular

songs? classical? jazz? "golden oldies"? Design an album cover and list three of your musical selections to accompany the scene segments. Indicate where in the scene you would insert these pieces.

4. Play directors keep notes about their ideas for a play in what is called a "prompt" book or log. In this book they write ideas about items such as scenery, costumes, lighting, speech cuts, stage directions and special effects. Begin your own prompt book or log for *A Midsummer Night's Dream*. Record ideas you have about the way this play should be presented in whatever order the ideas occur to you.

5. Bottom wants to be in the spotlight in the play Quince is directing. Helena wants to be a look-alike for Hermia. Egeus wants his daughter Hermia to behave as he wishes. Is this desire to be the all-powerful person or the most important person effective in developing good relationships with other people?

   In the Greek myth, *Narcissus*, a beautiful young man who rejected all the offers of love made to him was punished by being made to fall in love with his own image, which he was required to watch constantly in a pool of water. An Austrian psychiatrist named Sigmund Freud used the term *narcissism* to refer to a person who was totally absorbed with himself or herself.

   In your journal, describe the characteristics of someone you know or know about whom Freud might say is a victim of narcissism or is narcissistic. Explain whether you think narcissistic people are happy people and (where possible) support your ideas with evidence from your own experience or knowledge.

   Could any of the following characters be called narcissistic: Bottom, Helena, Egeus? Could any of the other characters in the play be accused of being totally self-absorbed? Talk about your ideas with a partner and report your opinions to your group.

34

6. Choose one of the characters, Lysander or Hermia, and write the letter the character might have written to a friend explaining why the couple have decided to flee Athens.

For the next scene . . .

What do you do when you feel torn between love and hate at the same time?

Act 2, Scene 1

In this scene. . .

This scene takes place at night in the forest that is ruled by Oberon and Titania, king and queen of the fairies. As the scene opens, we meet Puck, (Oberon's helpmate) and a fairy discussing the problems of the king and queen. Oberon and Titania are quarrelling about which one of them should have possession of a little boy, stolen from an Indian king. In order to get this child for himself, Oberon decides to use a love-potion on Titania which will make her fall in love with the first live creature she sees when she wakes from her sleep. Oberon will take charge of the boy while Titania is in this love-crazed condition, and then remove the effect of the potion from her. He sends Puck to find the flower with the magic love-juice.

As Puck leaves, Demetrius and Helena approach the forest. Helena begs Demetrius to love her, but Demetrius has eyes only for Hermia and is determined to find her. He orders Helena to leave him alone.

Oberon, observing the quarrel, decides to change the situation. When Puck returns with the love-potion, Oberon takes some of the juice to apply to Titania, and tells Puck to apply the rest of it to Demetrius so that he will love Helena.

1   *whither wander you?* where are you going?

3   *thorough:* through

4   *pale:* land enclosed by a fence (palings or pickets)

7   *the moon's sphere:* the moon's circle of movement. In Shakespeare's time, people believed that the moon moved and the earth stood still

9   *to dew . . . green:* to water the fairy rings (circles of darker grass that are actually forest fungi)

10   *cowslips:* a wildflower; *pensioners:* members of the royal bodyguard

12   *favours:* gifts

13   *savours:* perfumes

16   *lob of spirits:* clumsy clown. (This is an insult. Puck is bigger than the other fairies.)

17   *anon:* soon

18   *revels:* merrymaking

20   *passing fell and wrath:* very angry

21   *she:* Titania, the queen

23   *changeling:* a human child stolen by the fairies

25   *train:* followers; *trace:* wander through

26   *perforce:* by force

30   *square:* quarrel or argue

Act 2, Scene 1

A wood near Athens.

*Enter, from opposite sides, a Fairy
and Puck.*

Puck: How now, spirit! whither wander you?
Fairy: Over hill, over dale,
　　　Thorough bush, thorough brier,
　　　Over park, over pale,
　　Thorough flood, thorough fire, 5
I do wander everywhere,
Swifter than the moon's sphere;
And I serve the fairy queen,
To dew her orbs upon the green.
The cowslips tall her pensioners be: 10
In their gold coats spots you see;
Those be rubies, fairy favours,
In those freckles live their savours:
　I must go seek some dewdrops here
　And hang a pearl in every cowslip's ear. 15
　Farewell, thou lob of spirits; I'll be gone:
　Our queen and all her elves come here anon.
Puck: The king doth keep his revels here to-night:
　Take heed the queen come not within his sight;
　For Oberon is passing fell and wrath, 20
　Because that she as her attendant hath
　A lovely boy, stolen from an Indian king;
　She never had so sweet a changeling;
　And jealous Oberon would have the child
　Knight of his train to trace the forests wild; 25
　But she perforce withholds the loved boy,
　Crowns him with flowers, and makes him all her joy:
　And now they never meet in grove or green,
　By fountain clear, or spangled starlight sheen,
　But they do square, that all their elves for fear 30
　Creep into acorn cups and hide them there.

32   *mistake . . . quite:* don't recognize you

36   *Skim milk:* steal the cream from the milk; *labour in the quern:* play in the handmill for grinding grain

37   *And bootless . . . churn:* Because Puck is playing in the handmill, the woman is grinding away without any success.

38   *to bear no barm:* without yeast (barm), the beer (drink) will be flat

45   *beguile:* fool

46   *Neighing . . . foal:* imitating a female horse (mare)

47   *gossip's:* talkative woman's; *bowl:* drinking cup

48   *crab:* crab apples

50   *wither'd dewlap:* old, loose skin under the neck

54   *"tailor":* an obscure reference. It might mean she finds herself sitting cross-legged on the floor the way tailors sat to sew.

55   *quire:* choir. Here it means everyone who is listening to the woman's sad tale.

56   *waxen:* grow louder; *neeze:* sneeze – choking in their laughter

57   *wasted:* spent

58   *But, room, fairy!* loosely means ,"Look out!"

62   *forsworn:* given up

63   *rash wanton:* reckless, sexually immoral person

64-68   *Then I . . . Phillida:* Titania is asking Oberon why he flirts with another woman if she is his lady.

Fairy: Either I mistake your shape and making quite,
    Or else you are that shrewd and knavish sprite
    Call'd Robin Goodfellow: are not you he
    That frights the maidens of the villagery;   35
    Skim milk, and sometimes labour in the quern,
    And bootless make the breathless housewife churn;
    And sometime make the drink to bear no barm;
    Mislead night-wanderers, laughing at their harm?
    Those that Hobgoblin call you and sweet Puck,   40
    You do their work, and they shall have good luck:
    Are not you he?
Puck: Thou speak'st aright;
    I am that merry wanderer of the night.
    I jest to Oberon and make him smile
    When I a fat and bean-fed horse beguile,   45
    Neighing in likeness of a filly foal:
    And sometime lurk I in a gossip's bowl,
    In very likeness of a roasted crab,
    And when she drinks, against her lips I bob
    And on her wither'd dewlap pour the ale.   50
    The wisest aunt, telling the saddest tale,
    Sometime for three-foot stool mistaketh me;
    Then slip I from her and down topples she,
    And "tailor" cries, and falls into a cough;
    And then the whole quire hold their hips and laugh;   55
    And waxen in their mirth, and neeze, and swear
    A merrier hour was never wasted there.
    But, room, fairy! here comes Oberon.
Fairy: And here my mistress. Would that he were gone!

[*Enter, from one side, Oberon, with his train; from the other,*
    Titania with hers.]

Oberon: Ill met by moonlight, proud Titania.   60
Titania: What, jealous Obcron! Fairies, skip hence:
    I have forsworn his bed and company.
Oberon: Tarry, rash wanton: am not I thy lord?
Titania: Then I must be thy lady: but I know
    When thou hast stolen away from fairyland,   65
    And in the shape of Corin sat all day,
    Playing on pipes of corn and versing love

69   *steppe:* mountain range

70   *bouncing Amazon:* Hippolyta

71   *buskin'd:* wearing calf-length leather hunting boots

74-75 *Hot canst . . . Hippolyta:* How do you have the nerve to accuse me of flirting with Hippolyta?

77-80 *Didst thou . . . Antiopa:* Oberon accuses Titania of flirting with Theseus and of breaking up Theseus' romances with other women.

81   *forgeries of jealousy:* made-up stories because you are jealous

82   *the middle summer's spring:* the beginning of midsummer

85   *beachèd margent:* shore

86   *ringlets:* circular dances

90   *Contagious:* harmful, poisonous

91-92 *Have every . . . continents:* Even the smallest stream is so swollen with rain it has flooded its banks.

93-95 *The ox . . . beard:* The fields have been ploughed and planted for no reason because the rain has ruined everything

96-97 *The fold . . . flock:* The crows have gotten fat eating all the drowned sheep and diseased cattle.

98   *nine men's morris:* a dance. The area of land that is marked out for this dance has been washed away.

99-100 *And the quaint . . . undistinguishable:* The park walk-ways are overgrown with vegetation

101   *want their winter here:* are going without their usual winter festivities

105   *rheumatic diseases:* illnesses caused or made worse by dampness – coughs and colds

106   *distemperature:* disturbance in the natural order

> To amorous Phillida. Why art thou here,
> Come from the farthest steppe of India?
> But that, forsooth, the bouncing Amazon,   70
> Your buskin'd mistress and your warrior love,
> To Theseus must be wedded, and you come
> To give their bed joy and prosperity.

Oberon: How canst thou thus for shame, Titania,
>   Glance at my credit with Hippolyta,   75
> Knowing I know thy love to Theseus?
> Didst thou not lead him through the glimmering night
> From Perigenia, whom he ravished?
> And make him with fair Aegle break his faith,
> With Ariadne and Antiopa?   80

Titania: These are the forgeries of jealousy:
>   And never, since the middle summer's spring,
> Met we on hill, in dale, forest or mead,
> By pavèd fountain or by rushy brook,
> Or in the beachèd margent of the sea,   85
> To dance our ringlets to the whistling wind,
> But with thy brawls thou hast disturb'd our sport.
> Therefore the winds, piping to us in vain,
> As in revenge, have suck'd up from the sea
> Contagious fogs; which falling in the land   90
> Have every pelting river made so proud
> That they have overborne their continents:
> The ox hath therefore stretch'd his yoke in vain,
> The ploughman lost his sweat; and the green corn
> Hath rotted ere his youth attain'd a beard;   95
> The fold stands empty in the drowned field,
> And crows are fatted with the murrion flock;
> The nine men's morris is fill'd up with mud,
> And the quaint mazes in the wanton green
> For lack of tread are undistinguishable: 100
> The human mortals want their winter here;
> No night is now with hymn or carol blest:
> Therefore the moon, the governess of floods,
> Pale in her anger, washes all the air,
> That rheumatic diseases do abound: 105
> And thorough this distemperature we see
> The seasons alter: hoary-headed frosts

109   *Hiems:* the god of winter

110   *odorous chaplet:* sweet-smelling garland

112   *childing autumn:* fruitful or pregnant autumn – that is, harvest time

113   *wonted liveries:* usual clothing or appearance; *mazed:* amazed, or astonished

114   *by their increase:* by what the seasons are doing

115   *And this . . . comes:* all of these bad offspring or children

117   *original:* creators, cause

118   *amend it:* fix it

121   *henchman:* page-boy

123   *votaress:* a woman who had made a vow of service to Titania

126   *Neptune:* the god of the sea

127   *embarkèd traders:* merchant ships sailing off

142   *spare:* stay away from

145   *chide:* quarrel

Fall in the fresh lap of the crimson rose;
And on old Hiems' thin and icy crown
An odorous chaplet of sweet summer buds   110
Is, as in mockery, set: the spring, the summer,
The childing autumn, angry winter, change
Their wonted liveries, and the mazed world,
By their increase, now knows not which is which:
And this same progeny of evils comes   115
From our debate, from our dissension;
We are their parents and original.
Oberon: Do you amend it, then; it lies in you:
Why should Titania cross her Oberon?
I do but beg a little changeling boy,   120
To be my henchman.
Titania: Set your heart at rest:
The fairyland buys not the child of me.
His mother was a votaress of my order:
And, in the spicèd Indian air, by night,
Full often hath she gossip'd by my side,   125
And sat with me on Neptune's yellow sands,
Marking the embarkèd traders on the flood,
When we have laugh'd to see the sails conceive
And grow big-bellied with the wanton wind;
Which she, with pretty and with swimming gait   130
Following—her womb then rich with my young squire—
Would imitate, and sail upon the land,
To fetch me trifles, and return again,
As from a voyage, rich with merchandise.
But she, being mortal, of that boy did die;   135
And for her sake do I rear up her boy,
And for her sake I will not part with him.
Oberon: How long within this wood intend you stay?
Titania: Perchance till after Theseus' wedding-day.
If you will patiently dance in our round   140
And see our moonlight revels, go with us;
If not, shun me, and I will spare your haunts.
Oberon: Give me that boy, and I will go with thee.
Titania: Not for thy fairy kingdom. Fairies, away!
We shall chide downright, if I longer stay.   145

                         [Exit Titania with her train.]

147   *injury:* insult

151   *dulcet and harmonious breath:* sweet music

152   *rude:* rough

158   *vestal:* virgin. This line is probably a compliment to Queen Elizabeth I, also called the Virgin Queen.

161   *might:* was able to

162   *watery moon:* a reference to the fact that the moon controls the tides

163   *imperial votaress:* again, meaning Queen Elizabeth

164   *In maiden . . . free:* not in love with anyone because Cupid's arrow missed her

168   *love-in-idleness:* another name for pansy

174   *leviathan:* whale

175   *put a girdle round:* encircle, fly around

Oberon: Well, go thy way: thou shalt not from this grove
    Till I torment thee for this injury.
    My gentle Puck, come hither. Thou rememberest
    Since once I sat upon a promontory,
    And heard a mermaid on a dolphin's back   150
    Uttering such dulcet and harmonious breath
    That the rude sea grew civil at her song
    And certain stars shot madly from their spheres,
    To hear the sea-maid's music.
Puck: I remember.
Oberon: That very time I saw, but thou couldst not,   155
    Flying between the cold moon and the earth,
    Cupid all arm'd: a certain aim he took
    At a fair vestal thronèd by the west,
    And loosed his love-shaft smartly from his bow,
    As it should pierce a hundred thousand hearts;   160
    But I might see young Cupid's fiery shaft
    Quench'd in the chaste beams of the watery moon,
    And the imperial votaress passed on,
    In maiden meditation, fancy-free.
    Yet mark'd I where the bolt of Cupid fell: 165
    It fell upon a little western flower,
    Before milk-white, now purple with love's wound,
    And maidens call it love-in-idleness.
    Fetch me that flower; the herb I shew'd thee once:
    The juice of it on sleeping eyelids laid   170
    Will make or man or woman madly dote
    Upon the next live creature that it sees.
    Fetch me this herb; and be thou here again
    Ere the leviathan can swim a league.
Puck: I'll put a girdle round about the earth   175
    In forty minutes.   [*Exit.*]
Oberon: Having once this juice,
    I'll watch Titania when she is asleep,
    And drop the liquor of it in her eyes.
    The next thing then she waking looks upon,
    Be it on lion, bear, or wolf, or bull,   180
    On meddling monkey, or on busy ape,
    She shall pursue it with the soul of love:
    And ere I take this charm from off her sight,

As I can take it with another herb,
I'll make her render up her page to me. 185
But who comes here? I am invisible;
And I will overhear their conference.

[*Enter Demetrius, Helena following him.*]

Demetrius: I love thee not, therefore pursue me not.
Where is Lysander and fair Hermia?
The one I'll slay, the other slayeth me. 190
Thou told'st me they were stolen unto this wood;
And here am I, and wode within this wood,
Because I cannot meet my Hermia.
Hence, get thee gone, and follow me no more.
Helena: You draw me, you hard-hearted adamant; 195
But yet you draw not iron, for my heart
Is true as steel: leave you your power to draw,
And I shall have no power to follow you.
Demetrius: Do I entice you? do I speak you fair?
Or, rather, do I not in plainest truth 200
Tell you, I do not, nor I cannot love you?
Helena: And even for that do I love you the more.
I am your spaniel; and, Demetrius,
The more you beat me, I will fawn on you:
Use me but as your spaniel, spurn me, strike me, 205
Neglect me, lose me; only give me leave,
Unworthy as I am, to follow you.
What worser place can I beg in your love,—
And yet a place of high respect with me,—
Than to be usèd as you use your dog? 210
Demetrius: Tempt not too much the hatred of my spirit,
For I am sick when I do look on thee.
Helena: And I am sick when I look not on you.
Demetrius: You do impeach your modesty too much,
To leave the city and commit yourself 215
Into the hands of one that loves you not;
To trust the opportunity of night
And the ill counsel of a desert place
With the rich worth of your virginity.
Helena: Your virtue is my privilege: for that 220
It is not night when I do see your face,

227 *brakes:* bushes

230-234 *the story . . . valour flies:* in the usual course of events, Apollo chased the dove, the tiger chased the hind (deer). But Helena says to change the "story" because she – the woman – is chasing the man.

235 *stay thy questions:* listen to this

244 *upon:* by

255 *throws:* sheds

256 *Weed:* garment

Therefore I think I am not in the night;
Nor doth this wood lack worlds of company,
For you in my respect are all the world:
Then how can it be said I am alone,   225
When all the world is here to look on me?
Demetrius: I'll run from thee and hide me in the brakes,
    And leave thee to the mercy of wild beasts.
Helena: The wildest hath not such a heart as you.
    Run when you will, the story shall be changed: 230
    Apollo flies, and Daphne holds the chase;
    The dove pursues the griffin; the mild hind
    Makes speed to catch the tiger; bootless speed,
    When cowardice pursues and valour flies.
Demetrius: I will not stay thy questions; let me go: 235
    Or, if thou follow me, do not believe
    But I shall do thee mischief in the wood.
Helena: Ay, in the temple, in the town, the field,
    You do me mischief. Fie, Demetrius!
    Your wrongs do set a scandal on my sex: 240
    We cannot fight for love, as men may do;
    We should be woo'd and were not made to woo.
                                    [*Exit Demetrius.*]
    I'll follow thee and make a heaven of hell,
    To die upon the hand I love so well.   [*Exit.*]
Oberon: Fare thee well, nymph: ere he do leave this grove, 245
    Thou shalt fly him and he shall seek thy love.

[*Re-enter Puck.*]

Hast thou the flower there? Welcome, wanderer.
Puck: Ay, there it is.
Oberon: I pray thee, give it me.
    I know a bank where the wild thyme blows,
    Where oxlips and the nodding violet grows;   250
    Quite over-canopied with lush woodbine,
    With sweet musk-roses and with eglantine:
    There sleeps Titania sometime of the night,
    Lull'd in these flowers with dances and delight;
    And there the snake throws her enamell'd skin,   255
    Weed wide enough to wrap a fairy in:
    And with the juice of this I'll streak her eyes,

262 *espies:* looks on

265 *Effect:* perform

267 *cock crow:* the cock crows at dawn, when all supernatural beings must leave the human world. (Note that later in the play, in Act 3, Scene 2, lines 388-345, Oberon says that he and the other fairies are *not* confined to the hours of darkness.

And make her full of hateful fantasies.
Take thou some of it, and seek through this grove:
A sweet Athenian lady is in love   260
With a disdainful youth: anoint his eyes;
But do it when the next thing he espies
May be the lady: thou shalt know the man
By the Athenian garments he hath on.
Effect it with some care that he may prove   265
More fond on her than she upon her love:
And look thou meet me ere the first cock crow.
Puck: Fear not, my lord, your servant shall do so.
                                                    [*Exeunt.*]

Act 2, Scene 1: Activities

1. This scene gives the audience its first look at the forest. How does the forest look in your imagination? If you were the producer for this play, what materials would you use to create the effect you would like the forest to have on its audience?

2. In Titania's speech, lines 81-117, she refers to the unnatural effects her quarrel with Oberon is having on the physical environment. Think of someone whose behaviour has had a definite effect on you (positive or negative). Consider the effect of the behaviour as if it were one of the following:
   • a form of weather.
   • a vehicle in motion.
   • a colour.
   • an animal.
   • a musical instrument.
   • a form of your own choosing.

   In your journal, write about the way the person's behaviour affected your using the behaviour form you have selected.

   Refer to Titania's speech and see if any of the images she uses are similar to images you used.

3. Some of the characters in this scene are beginning to see themselves as animals rather than humans (see lines 117-185 and lines 202-210).

   How much of their behaviour comes as a result of them being in a forest setting? If you had to spend a long time in a forest, do you think you might begin to feel more like an animal than a human?

   Discuss your ideas in your group.

4. Are Titania and Oberon quarrelling with each other or are they trying to persuade each other to give in? With a partner, talk about your ideas.

   Imagine you must persuade a friend to clean up after a party you gave so that you can go to a movie. What kind of voice-tone would you use? Would you include body gestures? facial expressions? hand movements? If so, what form would they take? Would you use bribery? flattery?

   With a partner, role-play your persuasive techniques in front of your group. Decide who was most successful as a persuader and why. How can persuasion prevent an argument from occurring?

   Make a journal entry about your conclusions regarding persuasive techniques and their success in preventing quarrels.

5. What do you think Helena means when she says women "cannot fight for love, as men may do"? Do you agree with her? Why or why not?

   What is "the battle of the sexes"? Brainstorm your ideas.

   What do you think can or should be done about this battle?

   After you have discussed (argued, debated) your ideas, record your feelings about this issue in your journal.

For the next scene. . .

If you could offer advice to two couples where you observed that neither man loved the woman who loved him, and that both men loved the other woman, what might you say to them? What would you suggest they do?

Act 2, Scene 2

In this scene. . .

Nighttime falls in the forest and Oberon's spellbinding plans must move ahead quickly. Hermia and Lysander prepare for sleep. Oberon finds Titania and successfully casts a spell on her as she sleeps. Puck, in his haste to find Demetrius, becomes confused. Instead of casting a spell on Demetrius, he finds the other young man dressed in Athenian clothes and applies the love-juice to Lysander's eyes. As soon as Puck leaves, Helena and Demetrius enter. Lysander wakes up, sees Helena, and falls in love with her. Helena thinks Lysander is making fun of her and runs away, with Lysander following behind. Hermia is left alone and afraid.

1 *rounded:* dance in a circle

13 *Philomel:* In Greek mythology, Philomela was changed into a
   nightingale by the gods so she could escape the cruel torment
   of her brother.

Scene 2

Another part of the wood.

Enter Titania, with her train.

Titania: Come, now a roundel and a fairy song;
  Then, for the third part of a minute, hence;
  Some to kill cankers in the musk-rose buds,
  Some war with rere-mice for their leathern wings,
  To make my small elves coats, and some keep back   5
  The clamorous owl that nightly hoots and wonders
  At our quaint spirits. Sing me now asleep;
  Then to your offices and let me rest.

[*The Fairies sing.*]

First Fairy:
      You spotted snakes with double tongue,
        Thorny hedgehogs, be not seen;   10
      Newts and blind worms, do no wrong,
        Come not near our fairy queen.

[*Chorus.*]
      Philomel, with melody
      Sing in our sweet lullaby;
      Lulla, lulla, lullaby, lulla, lulla, lullaby: 15
        Never harm,
        Nor spell, nor charm,
      Come our lovely lady nigh;
      So, good night, with lullaby.

First Fairy:
      Weaving spiders, come not here;   20
        Hence you long-legg'd spinners, hence!
      Beetles black, approach not near;
        Worm nor snail, do no offence.

[*Chorus.*]
      Philomel, with melody, etc.

26 *sentinel:* guard

28 *Do it . . . take:* believe it is your true love

30 *ounce:* lynx

31 *pard:* leopard

32 *that:* whatever

36 *troth:* truthfully

38 *tarry:* wait

42 *one troth:* our single pledged faith

45 *Oh, take . . . innocence:* interpret my words as entirely innocent

46 *Love . . . conference:* Lovers should be able to understand each other.

52 *For . . . lie:* Sleeping beside you, I will not be false (that is, try anything.)

53 *riddles very prettily:* speaks skillfully

54-55 *Now much . . . lied:* loosely – What must you think of me if you think I called you a liar?

Second Fairy:
 Hence, away! now all is well: 25
 One aloof stand sentinel.
         [*Exeunt Fairies. Titania sleeps.*]

[*Enter Oberon, and squeezes the flower on Titania's eyelids.*]

Oberon: What thou seest when thou dost wake,
 Do it for thy true-love take,
 Love and languish for his sake:
 Be it ounce, or cat, or bear,   30
 Pard, or boar with bristled hair,
 In thy eye that shall appear
 When thou wakest, it is thy dear:
 Wake when some vile thing is near.   [*Exit.*]

[*Enter Lysander and Hermia.*]

Lysander: Fair love, you faint with wandering in the wood;   35
 And to speak troth, I have forgot our way:
 We'll rest us, Hermia, if you think it good,
 And tarry for the comfort of the day.
Hermia: Be it so, Lysander: find you out a bed;
 For I upon this bank will rest my head.   40
          [*She lies down.*]
Lysander: One turf shall serve as pillow for us both;
 One heart, one bed, two bosoms and one troth.
Hermia: Nay, good Lysander; for my sake, my dear,
 Lie further off yet, do not lie so near.
Lysander: Oh, take the sense, sweet, of my innocence!   45
 Love takes the meaning in love's conference.
 I mean, that my heart unto yours is knit
 So that but one heart we can make of it;
 Two bosoms interchained with an oath;
 So then two bosoms and a single troth.   50
 Then by your side no bed-room me deny;
 For lying so, Hermia, I do not lie.
Hermia: Lysander riddles very prettily:
 Now much beshrew my manners and my pride,
 If Hermia meant to say Lysander lied.   55
 But, gentle friend, for love and courtesy
 Lie further off; in human modesty,

68   *approve:* test

71   *weeds:* clothing

78   *Churl:* a boor

86   *darkling:* in the dark

Such separation as may well be said
Becomes a virtuous bachelor and a maid,
So far be distant; and, good night, sweet friend: 60
Thy love ne'er alter till thy sweet life end!
Lysander: Amen, amen, to that fair prayer, say I;
And then end life when I end loyalty!
          [He lies down some little way from Hermia.]
Here is my bed: sleep give thee all his rest!
Hermia: With half that wish the wisher's eyes be press'd! 65

[Enter Puck.]   *[They fall asleep.]*

Puck: Through the forest have I gone,
But Athenian found I none,
On whose eyes I might approve
This flower's force in stirring love.
Night and silence! Who is here? 70
Weeds of Athens he doth wear:
This is he, my master said,
Despisèd the Athenian maid;
And here the maiden, sleeping sound,
On the dank and dirty ground. 75
Pretty soul! she durst not lie
Near this lack-love, this kill-courtesy.
Churl, upon thy eyes I throw
All the power this charm doth owe.
When thou wakest, let love forbid 80
Sleep his seat on thy eyelid:
So awake when I am gone;
For I must now to Oberon.   *[Exit.]*

[Enter Demetrius and Helena, running.]

Helena: Stay, though thou kill me, sweet Demetrius.
Demetrius: I charge thee, hence, and do not haunt me thus. 85
Helena: O, wilt thou darkling leave me? do not so.
Demetrius: Stay, on thy peril; I alone will go.   *[Exit.]*
Helena: O, I am out of breath in this fond chase!
The more my prayer, the lesser is my grace.
Happy is Hermia, wheresoe'er she lies; 90
For she hath blessèd and attractive eyes.
How came her eyes so bright? Not with salt tears:

98   *dissembling glass of mine:* my lying mirror

99   *sphery eyne:* eyes as bright as stars

104   *Transparent:* bright and radiant

119   *And touching . . . skill:* and now that I am at the highest point
of human development

120   *marshal to:* director of

121   *o'erlook:* find, or read

123   *mockery:* ridicule

128   *flout my insufficiency:* laugh at me for not being able to get
Demetrius to love me

If so, my eyes are oftener wash'd than hers.
No, no, I am as ugly as a bear;
For beasts that meet me run away for fear:⠀⠀⠀⠀⠀⠀95
Therefore no marvel though Demetrius
Do, as a monster, fly my presence thus.
What wicked and dissembling glass of mine
Made me compare with Hermia's sphery eyne?
But who is here? Lysander! on the ground!⠀⠀⠀⠀100
Dead? or asleep? I see no blood, no wound.
Lysander, if you live, good sir, awake.
Lysander: [*Awaking*] And run through fire I will for thy sweet
⠀⠀sake.
Transparent Helena! Nature shows art,
That through thy bosom makes me see thy heart.⠀⠀105
Where is Demetrius? O, how fit a word
Is that vile name to perish on my sword!
Helena: Do not say so, Lysander; say not so.
What though he love your Hermia? Lord, what though?
Yet Hermia still loves you: then be content.⠀⠀⁄ 7S⠀⠀110
Lysander: Content with Hermia! No; I do repent
The tedious minutes I with her have spent.
Not Hermia but Helena I love:
Who will not change a raven for a dove?
• The will of man is by his reason sway'd⠀⠀⠀⠀115
And reason says you are the worthier maid.
Things growing are not ripe until their season:
So I, being young, till now ripe not to reason;
And touching now the point of human skill,
Reason becomes the marshal to my will⠀⠀⠀⠀120
And leads me to your eyes; where I o'erlook
Love's stories, written in love's richest book.⠀⁄ 7W
Helena: Wherefore was I to this keen mockery born?
When at your hands did I deserve this scorn?
Is't not enough, is't not enough, young man,⠀⠀⠀125
That I did never, no, nor never can,
Deserve a sweet look from Demetrius' eye,
But you must flout my insufficiency?
Good troth, you do me wrong, good sooth, you do,
In such disdainful manner me to woo.⠀⠀⠀⠀⠀130
But fare you well: perforce I must confess

137   *as a surfeit:* too much

139-140 *Or as . . . deceive:* No one is more against a belief than someone who used to believe in it.

151   *removed:* gone

154   *of all loves:* for love's sake

I thought you lord of more true gentleness.
O, that a lady, of one man refused,
Should of another therefore be abused!   [*Exit.*]
Lysander: She sees not Hermia. Hermia, sleep thou there: 135
And never mayst thou come Lysander near!
For as a surfeit of the sweetest things
The deepest loathing to the stomach brings,
Or as the heresies that men do leave
Are hated most of those they did deceive,   140
So thou, my surfeit and my heresy,
Of all be hated, but the most of me!
And, all my powers, address your love and might
To honour Helen and to be her knight!   [*Exit.*]
Hermia: [*Awaking*] Help me, Lysander, help me! do thy
    best   145
To pluck this crawling serpent from my breast!
Ay me, for pity! what a dream was here!
Lysander, look how I do quake with fear:
Methought a serpent eat my heart away,
And you sat smiling at his cruel prey.   150
Lysander! what, removed? Lysander! lord!
What, out of hearing? gone? no sound, no word?
Alack, where are you? speak, an if you hear,
Speak of all loves! I swoon almost with fear.
No? then I well perceive you are not nigh: 155
Either death or you I'll find immediately.   [*Exit.*]

Act 2, Scene 2: Activities

1. The bedtime songs that Titania has her attendants sing to her are for the purpose of warding off any evils in the forest. In groups, list the ways Oberon demonstrates his superior powers. What is his attitude when he reveals these powers? How does this make you feel about him?

2. Oberon, after placing a spell on Titania, orders her to wake up when something "vile" is near. Have you or someone you know ever tried to teach a friend a lesson by playing a practical joke on the person?

   Did the practical joke have the effect that was intended? Were there unexpected consequences? Would you or the person you know choose to teach a lesson again by playing a practical joke?

   Share your stories with your group.

3. Read your newspaper's horoscope section for a few days to see how horoscopes are written if you are not already familiar with their format. Then write out a horoscope for one of the four lovers, offering some suitable advice. Share your work with your group, and see if the others can guess who you have written about.

4. The spell that Puck has cast on Lysander has changed Lysander's earlier notions about love.

   Prepare a list of his ideas about love before he had the spell cast on him and a list of his ideas now that he is under the spell. In your group, compare the two lists, deciding which are the more desirable qualities.

   Create an ad for a product which can change Lysander's "before" feelings about love into his "after" feelings.

   Or

   Write a letter to Ann Landers giving her readers advice about what you think are "real" feelings of love.

5. Recall a nightmare you have had in which you were abandoned by friends and/or family. Describe the nightmare to a friend. You could act out your bad dream for your group.

   How did you feel when you woke up? Compare your feelings to the ones Hermia felt (lines 145-156). How were they similar to or different from hers?

   When Hermia dreamed of a snake eating her heart, she was imagining a picture that would take a real form. Lysander, her lover, is now under a spell and thinks that he is in love with Helena.

   Did your nightmare experience become reality? In your journal, record your ideas.

Act 2: Consider the Whole Act

1. Every character in Act 2 has a problem or is in some sort of difficulty. Choose one character and invent a product that might help the character solve his or her problem. For example, what product could help Helena win Demetrius' love? or Puck get his boss's instructions straight?

   With your group, brainstorm different approaches to selling the product. Discuss which sales pitch most suits the product you are creating.

   Write an advertisement for your product with other members of your group and videotape a 15-30 second commercial.

2. In today's movie industry, awards are given for special effects. If you were the director of A Midsummer Night's Dream, what one special effect would you feel was necessary when filming Act 2? In groups, present your ideas and choose the one you think is most effective. Select a scene segment in Act 2 and think of ways to make the special effect work.

You could present your scene to the class and discuss what worked and what didn't. Note the changes you would make if you did the scene again.

3. Many of the characters in this act have collisions similar to ones we see in movie car-chase scenes. You could convert a clash between two characters from this act into two cars in a chase and tape their argument using appropriate sound effects. Before you begin, decide whether you want to create a comical or sinister effect.

4. Demetrius uses threats to solve his problem with Helena. When you have attended or watched a sports event in which one or more persons threatened the official score-keeper, how did you feel about the angry threats? the people who were making them? Write a letter to the editor of a newspaper you know, giving your opinions on the use of rage or violence to solve human problems.

5. Elizabethan directors liked using special effects, especially musical ones, in plays they presented. A modern stage director of *A Midsummer Night's Dream* had characters in the forest scenes swing coloured plastic tubes as they spoke, making the stage forest hum with a mysterious sound. In your group, select a speech or parts of a speech to which you could add some background sound effects. Rehearse the lines, blending the sound effects with them and present the combination of words and special effects to members of your class.

For the next scene . . .

Who is your favourite comedian? What is it about his or her routine that makes you laugh?

Think about a play, movie, or commercial you have seen in which a character talked directly to the camera or audience rather than to the other actors. What effect did this action have on you? How did it affect your response to the rest of the performance? What function does this "direct contact" approach serve?

Act 3, Scene 1

In this scene . . .

Puck has put Titania into a dreamspell as Oberon instructed, and she lies asleep near the very spot in the forest where Bottom and his friends have come to rehearse the play "Pyramus and Thisbe." Like most play directors, Quince has all sorts of problems to deal with – complaints from his cast and disasters resulting from his attempts to create the play's special effects. Bottom assumes an authoritative voice explaining how the cast will have to reassure their audience that the lion in the play is only "pretend." Puck overhears Bottom and decides to test the cast's imagination by placing a real asshead on Bottom. The rest of the players run off in fear and confusion. Titania is awakened by the noise and immediately falls in love with a startled Bottom. What is he to make of her infatuation with him?

2   *pat, pat:* right on time

4   *tiring-house:* dressing room

7   *bully:* a friendly term meaning "good buddy"

12   *By'r lakin:* by our lady-kin or little lady, that is, the Virgin Mary
       – a mild oath; *parlous:* perilous, or dangerous

22   *written in eight and six:* written in the metre (or rhythm) of psalms
       and ballads – lines of eight syllables alternating with lines of six

Act 3, Scene 1

The wood. Titania lying asleep.

Enter Quince, Snug, Bottom,
Flute, Snout, and Starveling.

7ω

Bottom: Are we all met?
Quince: Pat, pat; and here's a marvellous convenient place
    for our rehearsal. This green plot shall be our stage,
    this hawthorn-brake our tiring-house; and we will do
it in action as we will do it before the duke.   5
Bottom: Peter Quince,—
Quince: What sayest thou, bully Bottom?
Bottom: There are things in this comedy of Pyramus and
    Thisby that will never please. First, Pyramus must draw
    a sword to kill himself; which the ladies cannot abide.   10
    How answer you that?
Snout: By'r lakin, a parlous fear.
Starveling: I believe we must leave the killing out, when all
    is done.
Bottom: Not a whit: I have a device to make all well. Write   15
    me a prologue; and let the prologue seem to say, we
    will do no harm with our swords and that Pyramus is
    not killed indeed; and, for the more better assurance,
    tell them that I Pyramus am not Pyramus, but Bottom
    the weaver: this will put them out of fear.   20
Quince: Well, we will have such a prologue; and it shall be
    written in eight and six.
Bottom: No, make it two more; let it be written in eight
    and eight.
Snout: Will not the ladies be afeared of the lion?   25
Starveling: I fear it, I promise you.
Bottom: Masters, you ought to consider with yourselves: to
    bring in—God shield us!—a lion among ladies, is a
    most dreadful thing; for there is not a more fearful wild-
    fowl than your lion living; and we ought to look to't.   30

36   *defect:* he means effect

39-40   *were pity of my life:* my life would be endangered

47   *almanac:* a calendar that also gives information about the sun, moon, tides, weather, and so on

53-55   *a bush of . . . Moonshine:* English peasants saw "the man in the moon" as carrying a bundle of sticks on his back.

54   *lanthorn:* lantern; *disfigure:* represent

61   *rough-cast:* plaster mixed with pebbles for coating the outside of buildings

Snout: Therefore another prologue must tell he is not a
    lion.
Bottom: Nay, you must name his name, and half his face
    must be seen through the lion's neck: and he himself
    must speak through, saying thus, or to the same   35
    defect,—"Ladies,"—or "Fair ladies,—I would wish
    you,"—or "I would request you,"—or "I would entreat
    you,—not to fear, not to tremble: my life for yours.
    If you think I come hither as a lion, it were pity of my
    life; no, I am no such thing; I am a man as other men   40
    are"; and there indeed let him name his name, and tell
    them plainly he is Snug the joiner.
Quince: Well, it shall be so. But there is two hard things;
    that is, to bring the moonlight into a chamber; for,
    you know, Pyramus and Thisby meet by moonlight.   45
Snout: Doth the moon shine that night we play our play?
Bottom: A calendar, a calendar! Look in the almanac; find
    out moonshine, find out moonshine.
Quince: Yes, it doth shine that night.
Bottom: Why, then may you leave a casement of the great   50
    chamber window, where we play, open, and the moon
    may shine in at the casement.
Quince: Ay; or else one must come in with a bush of thorns
    and a lanthorn, and say he comes to disfigure, or to
    present, the person of Moonshine. Then, there is   55
    another thing: we must have a wall in the great
    chamber; for Pyramus and Thisby, says the story, did
    talk through the chink of a wall.
Snout: You can never bring in a wall. What say you, Bottom?
Bottom: Some man or other must present Wall: and let him   60
    have some plaster, or some loam, or some rough-cast
    about him, to signify wall; and let him hold his fingers
    thus, and through that cranny shall Pyramus and
    Thisby whisper.
Quince: If that may be, then all is well. Come, sit down,   65
    every mother's son, and rehearse your parts. Pyramus,
    you begin: when you have spoken your speech, enter
    into that brake: and so every one according to his cue.

[*Enter Puck behind.*]

69   *hempen home-spuns:* country bumpkins wearing clothes of coarse fabric

71   *toward:* about to begin

87   *brisky juvenal:* lively young man; *eke:* also

90   *Ninus:* a mythical Assyrian king. This play takes place in Babylon, near Ninus' burial spot.

Puck: What hempen home-spuns have we swaggering here,
    So near the cradle of the fairy queen? 70
    What, a play toward! I'll be an auditor;
    An actor too perhaps, if I see cause.
Quince: Speak, Pyramus. Thisby, stand forth.
Bottom: Thisby, the flowers of odious savours sweet,—
Quince: Odours, odours. 75
Bottom: —odours savours sweet:
    So hath thy breath, my dearest Thisby dear.
    But hark, a voice! stay thou but here awhile,
    And by and by I will to thee appear.   [*Exit.*]
Puck: A stranger Pyramus than e'er played here.   [*Exit.*] 80
Flute: Must I speak now?
Quince: Ay, marry, must you; for you must understand he
    goes but to see a noise that he heard, and is to come
    again.
Flute: Most radiant Pyramus, most lily-white of hue, 85
    Of colour like the red rose on triumphant brier,
    Most brisky juvenal and eke most lovely Jew,
    As true as truest horse that yet would never tire,
    I'll meet thee, Pyramus, at Ninny's tomb.
Quince: "Ninus' tomb," man: why, you must not speak 90
    that yet; that you answer to Pyramus: you speak all your
    part at once, cues and all. Pyramus enter: your cue
    is past; it is, "never tire."
Flute: O,—as true as truest horse, that yet would never tire.

[*Re-enter Puck, and Bottom with an ass's head.*]

Bottom: If I were fair, Thisby, I were only thine. 95
Quince: O monstrous! O strange! we are haunted.
    Pray, masters! fly, masters! Help!
        [*Exeunt Quince, Snug, Flute, Snout, and Starveling.*]
Puck: I'll follow you, I'll lead you about a round,
    Through bog, through bush, through brake, through
      brier:
    Sometime a horse I'll be, sometime a hound, 100
      A hog, a headless bear, sometime a fire;
    And neigh, and bark, and grunt, and roar, and burn,
    Like horse, hound, hog, bear, fire at every turn.
                [*Exit.*]

104 *knavery:* a trick, or joke

107 *you see . . . own:* you've dreamed up something inside your own assinine head

109 *translated:* changed, transformed

122-123 *Whose note . . . nay:* a joke. A man hearing the cuckoo's song may think it is calling him a cuckold (a man whose wife is unfaithful to him).

128 *enamour'd of:* in love with

129 *enthralled to:* captivated with

130 *thy fair . . . perforce:* the power of your beauty

Bottom: Why do they run away? this is a knavery of them
to make me afeard.   105

[*Re-enter Snout.*]

Snout: O Bottom, thou art changed! what do I see on thee?
Bottom: What do you see? you see an ass-head of your own,
do you?   [*Exit Snout.*]

[*Re-enter Quince.*]

Quince: Bless thee, Bottom! bless thee! thou art translated.
[*Exit.*]

Bottom: I see their knavery: this is to make an ass of me;   110
to fright me, if they could. But I will not stir from this
place, do what they can: I will walk up and down here,
and I will sing, that they shall hear I am not afraid.
[*Sings.*]

> The ousel cock so black of hue,
>   With orange-tawny bill,   115
> The throstle with his note so true,
>   The wren with little quill,

Titania: [*Awaking*] What angel wakes me from my flowery
bed?
Bottom: [*Sings.*]

> The finch, the sparrow and the lark,   120
>   The plain-song cuckoo gray,
> Whose note full many a man doth mark,
>   And dares not answer nay:—

for indeed, who would set his wit to so foolish a bird?
who would give a bird the lie, though he cry "cuckoo"   125
never so?
Titania: I pray thee, gentle mortal, sing again:
Mine ear is much enamour'd of thy note;
So is mine eye enthralled to thy shape;
And thy fair virtue's force perforce doth move me   130
On the first view to say, to swear, I love thee.
Bottom: Methinks, mistress, you should have little reason
for that: and yet, to say the truth, reason and love
keep little company together now-a-days; the more the

136   *gleek upon occasion:* take a joke

148   *purge thy mortal grossness:* change you so that you are more like a fairy

pity that some honest neighbours will not make them　135
friends. Nay, I can gleek upon occasion.

Titania: Thou art as wise as thou art beautiful.

Bottom: Not so, neither: but if I had wit enough to get out
of this wood, I have enough to serve mine own turn.

Titania: Out of this wood do not desire to go:　140
Thou shalt remain here, whether thou wilt or no.
I am a spirit of no common rate:
The summer still doth tend upon my state;
And I do love thee: therefore, go with me;
I'll give thee fairies to attend on thee,　145
And they shall fetch thee jewels from the deep,
And sing while thou on pressed flowers dost sleep:
And I will purge thy mortal grossness so
That thou shalt like an airy spirit go.
Peaseblossom! Cobweb! Moth! and Mustardseed!　150

[*Enter Peaseblossom, Cobweb, Moth, and Mustardseed.*]

Peaseblossom: Ready,
Cobweb:　　　　　　And I.
Moth:　　　　　　　　And I.
Mustardseed:　　　　　　　And I.
All:　　　　　　　　　　Where shall we go?
Titania: Be kind and courteous to this gentleman;
Hop in his walks and gambol in his eyes;
Feed him with apricocks and dewberries,
With purple grapes, green figs, and mulberries;　155
The honey-bags steal from the humble-bees,
And for night-tapers crop their waxen thighs
And light them at the fiery glow-worm's eyes,
To have my love to bed and to arise;
And pluck the wings from painted butterflies　160
To fan the moonbeams from his sleeping eyes:
Nod to him, elves, and do him courtesies.

Peaseblossom: Hail, mortal!

Cobweb: Hail!

Moth: Hail!　165

Mustardseed: Hail!

Bottom: I cry your worships mercy, heartily: I beseech your
worship's name.

171-172 *if I cut . . . with you:* cobwebs were applied to cuts to stop bleeding

179-180 *I know . . . well:* this may be sarcasm because mustard is hot, not gentle or "patient"

186 *The moon . . . eye:* It looks like rain.

Cobweb: Cobweb.

Bottom: I shall desire you of more acquaintance, good Master 170
    Cobweb: if I cut my finger, I shall make bold with
    you. Your name, honest gentleman?

Peaseblossom: Peaseblossom.

Bottom: I pray you, commend me to Mistress Squash, your
    mother, and to Master Peascod, your father. Good 175
    Master Peaseblossom, I shall desire you of more
    acquaintance too. Your name, I beseech you, sir?

Mustardseed: Mustardseed.

Bottom: Good Master Mustardseed, I know your patience
well: that same cowardly, giant-like oxbeef hath 180
    devoured many a gentleman of your house: I promise
    you your kindred hath made my eyes water ere now.
    I desire your more acquaintance, good Master
    Mustardseed.

Titania: Come, wait upon him; lead him to my bower. 185
    The moon methinks looks with a watery eye;
    And when she weeps, weeps every little flower,
    Lamenting some enforced chastity.
    Tie up my love's tongue, bring him silently.

                                      [Exeunt.]

Act 3, Scene 1: Activities

1. In groups, discuss the slapstick potential of this scene. Choose a part of the scene to act out. You might wish to rewrite the lines in contemporary English. Rehearse your scene segment and present it to the class.

2. Bottom and his friends are concerned about not letting their play become too violent. In many movies today, directors, in their desire to present realistic situations, include violent and frightening scenes. Should violence be a part of the entertainment industry? Look through recent magazine and news articles to find material which both supports the use of violence in movies and argues against its use.

   In your group, discuss your feelings about violence shown on videos, in movie theatres and on TV shows.

3. In the last line of Scene 1, Titania says "Tie up my love's tongue, bring him silently." If you were the play's director, how would you suggest Titania deliver this line, jokingly or cruelly? What is your reasoning to support this choice?
   With a partner, role-play Titania rehearsing her last speech in this scene (lines 185-189).
   As the director, suggest ways in which Titania could emphasize selected lines.
   When you are both satisfied with the presentation, share the performance with others.

4. Bottom says that to play a "wall" you must put on a costume made of plaster and paint it with brick design. He wants to "personalize" the wall. What might a wall in one of the following places say if it could speak: your classroom; the gym; the cafeteria; a local shopping plaza; a room at home.

   Choose one and write a paragraph about "A Moment in the Life of a Wall."

5. Often writers compare objects or other people to a character so that they can communicate a personality trait of the character.

   If Helena was compared to a rock star, who might the rock star be? If Hermia was compared to an animal, which animal might it be?

6. In your director's prompt book (see page 34), write your responses to the following questions, explaining your answers.
   • Should Bottom's voice change pitch from the pitch he used in Act 2?
   • Should Titania and Bottom speak differently to each other than they do to other characters they talk with?
   • Should the fairies reveal their confusion about their queen's strange fascination with Bottom?

7. Titania prevents Bottom from leaving the wood and ties up his tongue to silence him. Why would she want to prevent him from speaking? How does her action make you feel about Titania?

   Why do you think Bottom let himself be used this way? Recall a story you have read, or heard about in which someone used terrorist actions to get his or her way.

   Was the terrorist's behaviour similar to or different from Titania's behaviour with Bottom? Were the victims' responses similar to or different from Bottom's?

   Write your opinion of what your community, provincial or federal government should do about acts of terrorism.

For the next scene . . .

Think of a time when you felt you were a victim of the actions of someone else. What events led to the incident? How did you react to being a victim? Knowing what you do now, how would you have handled the situation differently?

Act 3, Scene 2

In this scene . . .

Puck tells Oberon what he has been doing in the forest
and says that Titania has fallen in love with an ass.
Demetrius has found Hermia wandering about and
discovers that she thinks that he has killed Lysander.
Oberon realizes that Puck has put the juice in the
wrong man's eyes, and so he sprinkles the love juice
on Demetrius as soon as Demetrius falls asleep. Soon
Lysander and Helena come running in. Helena is still
convinced that Lysander is teasing her. Demetrius
wakes up and falls in love with Helena. Hermia now
enters and all four lovers have a nasty argument.
Demetrius and Lysander run off to fight and Helena
and Hermia run off in anger. Puck, at Oberon's bidding,
brings the four lovers back together again, and the
four fall asleep, exhausted. Puck then makes sure that
when they wake up, everyone will be in love with the
right person. Titania, who is still completely fascinated
with Bottom, has given Oberon the servant boy he
wanted. Now it's up to Oberon to respond . . .

3   *in extremity:* to the utmost degree

5   *night-rule:* "revels" or amusements

7   *close:* enclosed

9   *A crew . . . mechanicals:* a bunch of fools, of ignorant working-class people

10   *for bread:* for their living; *stalls:* shops, market booths

13   *shallowest thick-skin:* the stupidest (he means Bottom); *barren sort:* empty-headed, ridiculous group

17   *nole:* head

19   *my mimic:* the clown I'm talking about

21   *russet-pated choughs:* a sort of crow

28   *Made senseless . . . wrong:* they began running into things

Scene 2

Another part of the wood.

Enter Oberon.

Oberon: I wonder if Titania be awaked;
 Then, what it was that next came in her eye,
 Which she must dote on in extremity.

[*Enter Puck.*]

 Here comes my messenger.
                              How now, mad spirit!
 What night-rule now about this haunted grove?   5
Puck: My mistress with a monster is in love.
 Near to her close and consecrated bower,
 While she was in her dull and sleeping hour,
 A crew of patches, rude mechanicals,
 That work for bread upon Athenian stalls,   10
 Were met together to rehearse a play
 Intended for great Theseus' nuptial-day.
 The shallowest thick-skin of that barren sort,
 Who Pyramus presented, in their sport
 Forsook his scene, and enter'd in a brake: 15
 When I did him at this advantage take,
 An ass's nole I fixed on his head:
 Anon his Thisbe must be answered,
 And forth my mimic comes. When they him spy,
 As wild geese that the creeping fowler eye,   20
 Or russet-pated choughs, many in sort,
 Rising and cawing at the gun's report,
 Sever themselves and madly sweep the sky,
 So, at his sight, away his fellows fly;
 And, at our stamp, here o'er and o'er one falls;   25
 He murder cries and help from Athens calls.
 Their sense thus weak, lost with their fears thus strong,
 Made senseless things begin to do them wrong;

36   *latch'd:* anointed, or moistened

40   *of force:* of necessity

52-55   *I'll believe . . . Antipodes:* Hermia says it would be easier
        to believe that the moon could cut through the centre of the
        earth and shine during the day on the other side of the world.

61   *Venus:* the planet or star shining

For briers and thorns at their apparel snatch;
Some sleeves, some hats, from yielders all things catch.   30
I led them on in this distracted fear,
And left sweet Pyramus translated there:
When in that moment, so it came to pass,
Titania waked and straightway loved an ass.
Oberon: This falls out better than I could devise.   35
But hast thou yet latch'd the Athenian's eyes
With the love-juice, as I did bid thee do?
Puck: I took him sleeping,—that is finish'd too,—
And the Athenian woman by his side;
That, when he waked, of force she must be eyed.   40

[*Enter Hermia and Demetrius.*]

Oberon: Stand close: this is the same Athenian.
Puck: This is the woman, but not this the man.
Demetrius: O, why rebuke you him that loves you so?
Lay breath so bitter on your bitter foe.
Hermia: Now I but chide; but I should use thee worse,   45
For thou, I fear, hast given me cause to curse.
If thou hast slain Lysander in his sleep,
Being o'er shoes in blood, plunge in the deep,
And kill me too.
The sun was not so true unto the day   50
As he to me: would he have stolen away
From sleeping Hermia? I'll believe as soon
This whole earth may be bored and that the moon
May through the centre creep and so displease
Her brother's noontide with the Antipodes.   55
It cannot be but thou hast murder'd him;
So should a murderer look, so dead, so grim.
Demetrius: So should the murder'd look, and so should I,
Pierced through the heart with your stern cruelty:
Yet you, the murderer, look as bright, as clear,   60
As yonder Venus in her glimmering sphere.
Hermia: What's this to my Lysander? where is he?
Ah, good Demetrius, wilt thou give him me?
Demetrius: I had rather give his carcass to my hounds.
Hermia: Out, dog! out, cur! thou drivest me past the bounds   65
Of maiden's patience. Hast thou slain him, then?

71   *worm:* serpent

74   *You spend . . . mood:* you're wasting energy in mistaken anger

84-85   *So sorrow . . . owe:* I'm sadder because I'm so sleepy

90-91   *Of thy . . . true:* Out of your mistake it follows that you've messed up a true love and not fixed up the false one.

92-93   *Then fate . . . oath:* It is a law of fate that for every true lover there are a million that break their vows.

97   *sighs . . . dear:* Each sigh was thought to draw a drop of blood from the heart.

101   *Swifter . . . bow:* an expression meaning with great speed

Henceforth be never number'd among men!
O, once tell true, tell true, even for my sake!
Durst thou have look'd upon him being awake,
And hast thou kill'd him sleeping? O brave touch!   70
Could not a worm, an adder, do so much?
An adder did it; for with doubler tongue
Than thine, thou serpent, never adder stung.
Demetrius: You spend your passion on a misprised mood:
I am not guilty of Lysander's blood;   75
Nor is he dead, for aught that I can tell.
Hermia: I pray thee, tell me then that he is well.
Demetrius: An if I could, what should I get therefore?
Hermia: A privilege never to see me more.
And from thy hated presence part I so: 80
See me no more, whether he be dead or no.

                                            [Exit.]

Demetrius: There is no following her in this fierce vein:
Here therefore for a while I will remain.
So sorrow's heaviness doth heavier grow
For debt that bankrupt sleep doth sorrow owe;   85
Which now in some slight measure it will pay,
If for his tender here I make some stay.

                               [Lies down and sleeps.]

Oberon: What hast thou done? thou hast mistaken quite,
And laid the love-juice on some true love's sight:
Of thy misprision must perforce ensue   90
Some true love turn'd and not a false turn'd true.
Puck: Then fate o'errules, that, one man holding troth
A million fail, confounding oath on oath.
Oberon: About the wood go swifter than the wind,
And Helena of Athens look thou find;   95
All fancy-sick she is and pale of cheer,
With sighs of love, that costs the fresh blood dear:
By some illusion see thou bring her here:
I'll charm his eyes against she do appear.
Puck: I go, I go; look how I go,   100
Swifter than arrow from the Tartar's bow.   *[Exit.]*
Oberon: Flower of this purple dye,
        Hit with Cupid's archery,
        Sink in apple of his eye.

113   *a lover's fee:* a kiss

121   *preposterously:* outrageously

129   *When truth kills truth:* by twisting the truth, you're really lying

130   *These vows are Hermia's:* what you are saying to me should
       be said to Hermia

When his love he doth espy,   105
Let her shine as gloriously
As the Venus of the sky.
When thou wakest, if she be by,
Beg of her for remedy.

[*Re-enter Puck.*]

Puck: Captain of our fairy band,   110
Helena is here at hand;
And the youth, mistook by me,
Pleading for a lover's fee.
Shall we their fond pageant see?
Lord, what fools these mortals be!   115
Oberon: Stand aside: the noise they make
Will cause Demetrius to awake.
Puck: Then will two at once woo one;
That must needs be sport alone;
And those things do best please me   120
That befall preposterously.

[*Enter Lysander and Helena.*]

Lysander: Why should you think that I should woo in scorn?
Scorn and derision never come in tears:
Look, when I vow, I weep; and vows so born,
In their nativity all truth appears.   125
How can these things in me seem scorn to you,
Bearing the badge of faith, to prove them true?
Helena: You do advance your cunning more and more.
When truth kills truth, O devilish-holy fray!
These vows are Hermia's: will you give her o'er?   130
Weigh oath with oath, and you will nothing weigh:
Your vows to her and me, put in two scales,
Will even weigh, and both as light as tales.
Lysander: I had no judgment when to her I swore.
Helena: Nor none, in my mind, now you give her o'er.   135
Lysander: Demetrius loves her, and he loves not you.
Demetrius: [*Awaking*] O Helen, goddess, nymph, perfect,
divine!
To what, my love, shall I compare thine eyne?
Crystal is muddy. O, how ripe in show

141   *Taurus:* a range of mountains in Turkey

157   *A trim exploit:* a fine trick

160   *extort:* torture

166   *bequeath:* leave

169   *I will none:* I want none of her

171   *as guest-wise sojourn'd:* brief as a guest's visit

174   *Disparage . . . know:* Don't speak badly about something you
        know nothing about. (He means his love for Helena.)

175   *aby it dear:* pay for it at great cost

Thy lips, those kissing cherries, tempting grow! 140
That pure congealed white, high Taurus' snow,
Fann'd with the eastern wind, turns to a crow
When thou hold'st up thy hand: O, let me kiss
This princess of pure white, this seal of bliss!
Helena: O spite! O hell! I see you all are bent 145
To set against me for your merriment:
If you were civil and knew courtesy,
You would not do me thus much injury.
Can you not hate me, as I know you do,
But you must join in souls to mock me too? 150
If you were men, as men you are in show,
You would not use a gentle lady so;
To vow, and swear, and superpraise my parts,
When I am sure you hate me with your hearts.
You both are rivals, and love Hermia; 155
And now both rivals, to mock Helena:
A trim exploit, a manly enterprise,
To conjure tears up in a poor maid's eyes
With your derision! none of noble sort
Would so offend a virgin and extort 160
A poor soul's patience, all to make you sport.
Lysander: You are unkind, Demetrius; be not so;
For you love Hermia; this you know I know:
And here, with all good will, with all my heart,
In Hermia's love I yield you up my part; 165
And yours of Helena to me bequeath,
Whom I do love and will do till my death.
Helena: Never did mockers waste more idle breath.
Demetrius: Lysander, keep thy Hermia; I will none:
If e'er I loved her, all that love is gone. 170
My heart to her but as guest-wise sojourn'd,
And now to Helen is it home return'd,
There to remain.
Lysander: Helen, it is not so.
Demetrius: Disparage not the faith thou dost not know,
Lest, to thy peril, thou aby it dear. 175
Look, where thy love comes; yonder is thy dear.

[*Re-enter Hermia.*]

177 *Dark . . . takes:* night takes away the ability to see

178-180 *The ear . . . recompense:* Your hearing becomes better when you can't see.

187 *engilds:* brightens

188 *oes and eyes:* stars

192 *confederacy:* conspiracy

193-194 *Now I . . . of me:* I know the three of them have ganged up to make a game of teasing me.

195 *injurious:* hurtful

203 *artificial gods:* creative people

205 *sampler:* a piece of embroidery

208 *incorporate:* joined together

213 *heraldry:* the art of designing a coat-of-arms that symbolizes a family motto

Hermia: Dark night, that from the eye his function takes,
   The ear more quick of apprehension makes;
   Wherein it doth impair the seeing sense,
   It pays the hearing double recompense.   180
   Thou art not by mine eye, Lysander, found;
   Mine ear, I thank it, brought me to thy sound.
   But why unkindly didst thou leave me so?
Lysander: Why should he stay, whom love doth press to
   go?
Hermia: What love could press Lysander from my side?   185
Lysander: Lysander's love, that would not let him bide
   Fair Helena, who more engilds the night
   Than all yon fiery oes and eyes of light.
   Why seek'st thou me? could not this make thee know,
   The hate I bear thee made me leave thee so?   190
Hermia: You speak not as you think: it cannot be.
Helena: Lo, she is one of this confederacy!
   Now I perceive they have conjoin'd all three
   To fashion this false sport, in spite of me.
   Injurious Hermia! most ungrateful maid!   195
   Have you conspired, have you with these contrived
   To bait me with this foul derision?
   Is all the counsel that we two have shared,
   The sisters' vows, the hours that we have spent,
   When we have chid the hasty-footed time   200
   For parting us,—O, is all forgot?
   All school-days' friendship, childhood innocence?
   We, Hermia, like two artificial gods,
   Have with our needles created both one flower,
   Both on one sampler, sitting on one cushion,   205
   Both warbling of one song, both in one key,
   As if our hands, our sides, voices and minds,
   Had been incorporate. So we grew together,
   Like to a double cherry, seeming parted,
   But yet an union in partition;   210
   Two lovely berries moulded on one stem;
   So, with two seeming bodies, but one heart;
   Two of the first, like coats in heraldry,
   Due but to one and crowned with one crest.
   And will you rend our ancient love asunder,   215

230   *tender:* offer, give

237   *counterfeit:* fake

238   *Make mouths upon me:* make faces at me

240   *chronicled:* recorded. She is being sarcastic when she says their teasing is important enough to be written down.

242   *argument:* target (for your jokes)

248   *If she . . . compel:* Speaking to Lysander, Demetrius tells him that if Hermia can't plead with him to leave Helena alone, he (Demetrius) will force him to.

To join with men in scorning your poor friend?
It is not friendly, 'tis not maidenly:
Our sex, as well as I, may chide you for it,
Though I alone do feel the injury.

Hermia: I am amazed at your passionate words. 220
I scorn you not: it seems that you scorn me.

Helena: Have you not set Lysander, as in scorn,
To follow me and praise my eyes and face?
And made your other love, Demetrius,
Who even but now did spurn me with his foot, 225
To call me goddess, nymph, divine and rare,
Precious, celestial? Wherefore speaks he this
To her he hates? and wherefore doth Lysander
Deny your love, so rich within his soul,
And tender me, forsooth, affection, 230
But by your setting on, by your consent?
What though I be not so in grace as you,
So hung upon with love, so fortunate,
But miserable most, to love unloved?
This you should pity rather than despise. 235

* *Hermia:* I understand not what you mean by this.

Helena: Ay, do, persever, counterfeit sad looks,
Make mouths upon me when I turn my back;
Wink each at other; hold the sweet jest up:
This sport, well carried, shall be chronicled. 240
If you have any pity, grace, or manners,
You would not make me such an argument.
But fare ye well: 'tis partly my own fault;
Which death or absence soon shall remedy.

Lysander: Stay, gentle Helena; hear my excuse: 245
My love, my life, my soul, fair Helena!

Helena: O excellent!

Hermia: Sweet, do not scorn her so.

Demetrius: If she cannot entreat, I can compel.

Lysander: Thou canst compel no more than she entreat:
Thy threats have no more strength than her weak prayers. 250
Helen, I love thee; by my life, I do:
I swear by that which I will lose for thee,
To prove him false that says I love thee not.

Demetrius: I say I love thee more than he can do.

103

258   *Ethiope:* person of dark complexion

262   *Tartar:* person of dark complexion

274   *erewhile:* before

288   *puppet:* a doll or toy, and not a real woman

Lysander: If thou say so, withdraw, and prove it too.　　　255
Demetrius: Quick, come!
Hermia:　　　　　　　Lysander, whereto tends all this?
Lysander: Away, you Ethiope!
Demetrius:　　　　　　　No, no; he'll——
　Seem to break loose; take on as you would follow,
　But yet come not: you are a tame man, go!
Lysander: Hang off, thou cat, thou burr! vile thing, let loose,　260
　Or I will shake thee from me like a serpent!
Hermia: Why are you grown so rude? what change is this?
　Sweet love,—
Lysander:　　　Thy love! out, tawny Tartar, out!
　Out, loathed medicine! hated potion, hence!
Hermia: Do you not jest?
Helena:　　　　　　　Yes, sooth; and so do you.　　　265
Lysander: Demetrius, I will keep my word with thee.
Demetrius: I would I had your bond, for I perceive
　A weak bond holds you: I'll not trust your word.
Lysander: What, should I hurt her, strike her, kill her dead?
　Although I hate her, I'll not harm her so.　　　270
Hermia: What, can you do me greater harm than hate?
　Hate me! wherefore? O me, what news, my love!
　Am not I Hermia? are not you Lysander?
　I am as fair now as I was erewhile.
　Since night you loved me; yet since night you left me:　275
　Why, then you left me—O, the gods forbid!—
　In earnest, shall I say?
Lysander:　　　　　　　Ay, by my life;
　And never did desire to see thee more.
　Therefore be out of hope, of question, of doubt;
　Be certain, nothing truer; 'tis no jest　　　280
　That I do hate thee and love Helena.
Hermia: O me! you juggler! you canker-blossom!
　You thief of love; what, have you come by night
　And stolen my love's heart from him?.
Helena:　　　　　　　Fine, i' faith!
　Have you no modesty, no maiden shame,　　　285
　No touch of bashfulness? What, will you tear
　Impatient answers from my gentle tongue?
　Fie, fie! you counterfeit, you puppet, you!

291   *urged:* boasted about

292   *personage:* figure

312   *chid me hence:* ordered me to leave

324   *vixen:* shrew (literally, she-fox)

Hermia: Puppet? why so? ay, that way goes the game.
  Now I perceive that she hath made compare   290
  Between our statures; she hath urged her height;
  And with her personage, her tall personage,
  Her height, forsooth, she hath prevail'd with him.
  And are you grown so high in his esteem,
  Because I am so dwarfish and so low?   295
  How low am I, thou painted maypole? speak;
  How low am I? I am not yet so low
  But that my nails can reach unto thine eyes. /
Helena: I pray you, though you mock me, gentlemen,
  Let her not hurt me: I was never curst;   300
  I have no gift at all in shrewishness;
  I am a right maid for my cowardice:
  Let her not strike me. You perhaps may think,
  Because she is something lower than myself,
  That I can match her.
Hermia: Lower! hark, again.   305
Helena: Good Hermia, do not be so bitter with me.
  I evermore did love you, Hermia,
  Did ever keep your counsels, never wrong'd you;
  Save that, in love unto Demetrius,
  I told him of your stealth unto this wood.   310
  He follow'd you; for love I follow'd him;
  But he hath chid me hence and threaten'd me
  To strike me, spurn me, nay, to kill me too:
  And now, so you will let me quiet go,
  To Athens will I bear my folly back   315
  And follow you no further: let me go:
  You see how simple and how fond I am.
Hermia: Why, get you gone: who is't that hinders you?
Helena: A foolish heart, that I leave here behind.
Hermia: What, with Lysander?
Helena: With Demetrius.   320
Lysander: Be not afraid; she shall not harm thee, Helena.
Demetrius: No, sir, she shall not, though you take her part.
Helena: O, when she's angry, she is keen and shrewd!
  She was a vixen when she went to school;
  And though she be but little, she is fierce.   325
Hermia: Little again! nothing but low and little!

329 *minimus:* a tiny creature; *knot-grass:* a weed that was thought to stunt the growth of children and animals

330 *officious:* obliging, eager to serve

333-335 *if thou . . . aby it:* if you offer her even the smallest sign of love, you'll pay for it

338 *cheek by jole:* side-by-side (literally, cheek by jaw)

339 *coil:* uproar, trouble; *'long of you:* because of you

352 *sort:* turn out

353 *jangling:* quarrelling

356 *welkin:* sky

357 *Acheron:* a river in Hades (Hell)

358 *testy:* headstrong or argumentative (from the French word for head, *tête*)

360 *Like to . . . tongue:* make yourself sound like Lysander sometimes

Why will you suffer her to flout me thus?
Let me come to her.
Lysander: Get you gone, you dwarf;
 You minimus, of hindering knot-grass made;
 You bead, you acorn.
Demetrius: You are too officious   330
 In her behalf that scorns your services.
 Let her alone: speak not of Helena;
 Take not her part; for, if thou dost intend
 Never so little show of love to her,
 Thou shalt aby it.
Lysander: Now she holds me not;   335
 Now follow, if thou darest, to try whose right,
 Of thine or mine, is most in Helena.
Demetrius: Follow! nay, I'll go with thee, cheek by jole.
      [Exeunt Lysander and Demetrius.]
Hermia: You, mistress, all this coil is 'long of you:
 Nay, go not back.
Helena: I will not trust you, I,   340
 Nor longer stay in your curst company.
 Your hands than mine are quicker for a fray,
 My legs are longer though, to run away. *[Exit.]*
Hermia: I am amazed, and know not what to say.
              [Exit.]
Oberon: This is thy negligence: still thou mistakest, 345
 Or else committ'st thy knaveries wilfully.
Puck: Believe me, king of shadows, I mistook.
 Did not you tell me I should know the man
 By the Athenian garments he had on?
 And so far blameless proves my enterprise, 350
 That I have 'nointed an Athenian's eyes;
 And so far am I glad it so did sort,
 As this their jangling I esteem a sport.
Oberon: Thou see'st these lovers seek a place to fight:
 Hie therefore, Robin, overcast the night; 355
 The starry welkin cover thou anon
 With drooping fog as black as Acheron;
 And lead these testy rivals so astray
 As one come not within another's way.
 Like to Lysander sometime frame thy tongue, 360

362 *rail:* yell and cry

369 *wonted:* usual

372 *wend:* go, travel

373 *With league . . . end:* with a close friendship until death

380 *Aurora's harbinger:* the morning star (Aurora – the dawn; harbinger – the announcer)

389 *I with . . . sport:* Oberon may mean that he has often enjoyed the pleasures of the dawn, instead of being driven off by it.

Then stir Demetrius up with bitter wrong;
And sometime rail thou like Demetrius;
And from each other look thou lead them thus,
Till o'er their brows death-counterfeiting sleep
With leaden legs and batty wings doth creep: 365
Then crush this herb into Lysander's eye;
Whose liquor hath this virtuous property,
To take from thence all error with his might,
And make his eyeballs roll with wonted sight,
When they next wake, all this derision 370
Shall seem a dream and fruitless vision,
And back to Athens shall the lovers wend,
With league whose date till death shall never end.
Whiles I in this affair do thee employ,
I'll to my queen and beg her Indian boy; 375
And then I will her charmèd eye release
From monster's view, and all things shall be peace.
Puck: My fairy lord, this must be done with haste,
For night's swift dragons cut the clouds full fast,
And yonder shines Aurora's harbinger, 380
At whose approach, ghosts, wandering here and there,
Troop home to churchyards: damnèd spirits all,
That in crossways and floods have burial,
Already to their wormy beds are gone;
For fear lest day should look their shames upon, 385
They wilfully themselves exile from light
And must for aye consort with black-brow'd night.
Oberon: But we are spirits of another sort:
I with the morning's love have oft made sport,
And, like a forester, the groves may tread, 390
Even till the eastern gate, all fiery-red,
Opening on Neptune with fair blessèd beams,
Turns into yellow gold his salt green streams.
But, notwithstanding, haste; make no delay:
We may effect this business yet ere day. [*Exit.*] 395
Puck: Up and down, up and down,
        I will lead them up and down:
        I am fear'd in field and town:
        Goblin, lead them up and down.

Here comes one. 400

111

402   *drawn:* with my sword out

409   *recreant:* coward

412   *we'll try . . . here:* We won't test our courage (or masculine strength) here.

[*Re-enter Lysander.*]

Lysander: Where art thou, proud Demetrius? speak thou
    now.
Puck: Here, villain; drawn and ready. Where art thou?
Lysander: I will be with thee straight.
Puck: Follow me, then,
    To plainer ground.
              [*Exit Lysander, as following the voice.*]

[*Re-enter Demetrius.*]

Demetrius: Lysander! speak again:
    Thou runaway, thou coward, art thou fled?   405
    Speak! In some bush? Where dost thou hide thy head?
Puck: Thou coward, art thou bragging to the stars,
    Telling the bushes that thou look'st for wars,
    And wilt not come? Come, recreant; come, thou child;
    I'll whip thee with a rod: he is defiled   410
    That draws a sword on thee.
Demetrius: Yea, art thou there?
Puck: Follow my voice: we'll try no manhood here.
                          [*Exeunt.*]

[*Re-enter Lysander.*]

Lysander: He goes before me and still dares me on:
    When I come where he calls, then he is gone.
    The villain is much lighter-heel'd than I: 415
    I follow'd fast, but faster he did fly;
    That fallen am I in dark uneven way,
    And here will rest me. [*Lies down.*] Come, thou gentle
      day!
    For if but once thou show me thy grey light,
    I'll find Demetrius and revenge this spite.   [*Sleeps.*] 420

[*Re-enter Puck and Demetrius.*]

Puck: Ho, ho, ho! Coward, why comest thou not?
Demetrius: Abide me, if thou darest; for well I wot
    Thou runn'st before me, shifting every place,
    And darest not stand, nor look me in the face.
    Where art thou now?

432   *abate:* shorten

435-436 *And sleep . . . company:* And may sleep let me forget

Puck: Come hither: I am here.   425
Demetrius: Nay, then, thou mock'st me. Thou shalt buy
   this dear,
   If ever I thy face by daylight see:
   Now, go thy way. Faintness constraineth me
   To measure out my length on this cold bed.
   By day's approach look to be visited.   430
                                   [*Lies down and sleeps.*]

[*Re-enter Helena.*]

Helena: O weary night, O long and tedious night,
   Abate thy hours! Shine comforts from the east,
   That I may back to Athens by daylight,
      From these that my poor company detest:
   And sleep, that sometimes shuts up sorrow's eye,   435
   Steal me awhile from mine own company.
                                   [*Lies down and sleeps.*]
Puck: Yet but three? Come one more;
           Two of both kinds makes up four.
           Here she comes, curst and sad:
           Cupid is a knavish lad,   440
           Thus to make poor females mad.

[*Re-enter Hermia.*]

Hermia: Never so weary, never so in woe:
   Bedabbled with the dew and torn with briers,
   I can no further crawl, no further go;
      My legs can keep no pace with my desires.   445
   Here will I rest me till the break of day.
   Heavens shield Lysander, if they mean a fray!
                                   [*Lies down and sleeps.*]
Puck: On the ground
                 Sleep sound:
                 I'll apply   450
                 To your eye,
           Gentle lover, remedy.
                 [*Squeezing the juice on Lysander's eyes.*]
                 When thou wakest,
                 Thou takest
                 True delight   455

461   *Jack . . . Jill:* a proverb (short well-known saying) meaning that every man should have his woman

In the sight
Of thy former lady's eye:
And the country proverb known,
That every man should take his own,
In your waking shall be shown: 460
    Jack shall have Jill;
    Nought shall go ill;
The man shall have his mare again, and all shall be well.

[Exit.]

Act 3, Scene 2: Activities

1. Puck usually expresses himself poetically. What main personality trait do you associate with him? What song or poem do you know that you could connect with his personality?

2. At the beginning of the scene (lines 6-34), Puck tells Oberon what has been happening in the wood. Because the audience has already seen these events, Shakespeare had to write the speech so the audience wouldn't become bored. What did Shakespeare have Puck do to maintain audience interest?

   Experiment with performing Puck's speech. One way you might consider is by using Chamber theatre.

   In Chamber theatre, a story-teller delivers his or her own thoughts and feelings, while the other actors perform the lines that refer to them. The story-teller may move among the actors while expressing his or her thoughts and feelings but can't be watched by the actors. The actors may perform their lines by saying the words, using actions, or combining the two.

   In a group, practise Puck's speech and present it to other groups when you are ready.

3. In lines 110-121, Puck refers to the mix-up of the four lovers as a "pageant" (entertainment) and admits that he enjoys watching muddled-up situations. How would you describe someone who finds humour in these circumstances?

   When have you or has someone you know acted like Puck? (You may wish to reread Act 2, Scene 1, lines 32-58 to recall another example of his behaviour.)

   In your journal, write an entry in which you describe how you behaved and what were the results of your behaviour.

4. The intense power-struggle between Hermia-Helena and Lysander-Demetrius has led to an identity crisis for Hermia – "Am I not Hermia?" (line 273). How did Hermia think of herself in Acts 1 and 2? Compare her feelings in previous acts to the way she feels about herself now. Why do you think she feels so threatened?

5. Lysander and Demetrius decide to fight each other to see who loves Helena more. How do you feel about people having physical fights to demonstrate or prove their love for a third person?

   Write an article for a newspaper you know exploring the topic of "fighting" for "love." Before you begin the article, decide whether you want it to be humorous or serious.

6. In a group of four, select a part (or all) of the fight scene between the lovers (lines 122-344) and prepare it for presentation to the class. Consider the following before you begin this activity:
   • Will you rewrite the lines in modern dialogue or use the Shakespearean language?
   • Will you give it a modern setting or stay with the play setting?
   • What main aspect(s) of the argument will you emphasize?
   • What main idea do you wish to communicate to your audience?

   Rehearse your scene segment until you feel comfortable with your dialogue and actions.

Act 3: Consider the Whole Act

1. We know that, because of a potion, Titania has taken one look at Bottom and fallen in love with him. Lysander and Demetrius for the same reason have suddenly fallen in love with Helena. In real life, without the effect of potions, people sometimes fall in love "at first sight" with the looks of the other person, without knowing about the person.

In your journal, describe a couple you know who have fallen in love this way. At the end of your entry, write your ideas about love, explaining what would be most important to you if you fell in love with someone.

2. By this point in the play, you have probably identified major areas of concern related to the development of the story-line. In your group, have each member think of a question he or she would like answered. You might pose your question by saying, "What I want to know is: What . . .? When . . .? Where . . .? Why . . .? How . . .?"

After you have discussed the questions and your answers to them, make any notes that might assist you in understanding the continuing story-line for the play.

3. You have seen how Bottom was changed completely. What other examples of *metamorphosis* can you recall from fairy tales or myths you remember? Have you ever had a friend or known a person or popular entertainer who had a metamorphosis? How did the person feel about his or her change afterwards? (If you don't know, imagine what effect the total change had on the person.) Talk about your ideas in your group.

As a cartoonist, plan a comic strip in which a character undergoes a complete change.

What age is your character? Where does the change take place? What new powers could the character have. What ages are the audience for your comic strip?

Was the metamorphosis wished for by your character or did a mysterious force make the change secretly? Were the results humorous or disastrous?

4. Select a speech in this act that you particularly like and rehearse it for presentation. Decide what is the main idea and feeling of the speech, and how you will communicate both. Your goal is to have your audience hear and feel your message. As you practise your speech, keep the following in mind: speak loudly and clearly; don't hurry

your lines; move naturally and freely; become your character.

Present your speech to other members of your class.

5. The play takes place in a mythical Greek setting both in the palace of the Greek hero, Theseus, and in a wooded place near Athens. If you were designing the costumes for the three groups of characters (the people of the palace, the workmen, and the fairies), what kinds of costumes would you give each group?

   Would you give any of the groups clothing from styles found in the following times: ancient Greek times? early Roman times? the Elizabethan period? modern times?

   In your group, decide what costumes you would use and share your choices with ones made by other groups.

For the next scene . . .

Have you ever had a dream that was so realistic and moving that you found it hard to believe it was only a dream? In your journal, describe the dream, explaining what kind of effect it had on you.

If you have not had this experience, think of a dream someone you know or know of had that was similar and describe it.

Act 4, Scene 1

In this scene . . .

Oberon watches as Titania and the fairies entertain
Bottom. When she and Bottom fall asleep, Oberon tells
Puck that Titania has given him the servant-child and
so he will now release her from the spell. Titania
awakes, wondering why she was in love with an
ass. Oberon then tells Puck to take the asshead off
Bottom. He predicts that Lysander and Hermia and
Demetrius and Helena will be married on the same day
that Theseus and Hippolyta are married. The four
lovers, who are asleep, are discovered by Theseus,
Hippolyta, and Egeus when they enter the forest on
a hunt. Lysander explains to Theseus why he and
Hermia are in the forest. Egeus, hearing that the couple
were trying to flee the Athenian law, demands punish-
ment for Lysander. Theseus overrules Egeus' will
however, and announces that the young Athenian lovers
will be married at his own wedding ceremony.

After the hunting party and the lovers leave the forest
to return to Athens, Bottom wakes up trying to make
some sense of his "dream."

2   *amiable:* lovely; *coy:* caress

16   *oerflown with:* covered with

19   *neaf:* fist

20   *leave your courtesy:* stop bowing to me

22   *Cavalery:* cavalier or gallant

Act 4, Scene 1

*The same. Lysander, Demetrius,
Helena, and Hermia lying asleep.*

*Enter Titania and Bottom;
Peaseblossom, Cobweb, Moth,
Mustardseed, and other Fairies
attending; Oberon behind unseen.*

Titania:
Come sit thee down upon this flowery bed,
   While I thy amiable cheeks do coy,
And stick musk-roses in thy sleek smooth head,
   And kiss thy fair large ears, my gentle joy.
Bottom: Where's Peaseblossom?   5
Peaseblossom: Ready.
Bottom: Scratch my head, Peaseblossom. Where's Mounsieur
   Cobweb?
Cobweb: Ready.
Bottom: Mounsieur Cobweb, good mounsieur, get you your   10
   weapons in your hand, and kill me a red-hipped
   humble-bee on the top of a thistle; and, good
   mounsieur, bring me the honey-bag. Do not fret
   yourself too much in the action, mounsieur; and, good
   mounsieur, have a care the honey-bag break not; I   15
   would be loath to have you overflown with a honey-bag,
   signior. Where's Mounsieur Mustardseed?
Mustardseed: Ready.
Bottom: Give me your neaf, Mounsieur Mustardseed.
   Pray you, leave your courtesy, good mounsieur.   20
Mustardseed: What's your will?
Bottom: Nothing, good mounsieur, but to help Cavalery
   Cobweb to scratch. I must to the barber's, mounsieur;
   for methinks I am marvellous hairy about the face; and
   I am such a tender ass, if my hair do but tickle me,   25
   I must scratch.

29   *tongs and the bones:* simple musical instruments. Tongs were hit with a piece of metal (like a triangle), and the bones were rattled between the fingers.

31   *a peck of provender:* a quantity of food such as hay or corn (animal feed)

32   *bottle:* bundle

33   *fellow:* equal

38   *exposition:* blunder for disposition. Bottom has the desire to sleep.

46   *dotage:* obsession

48   *this hateful fool:* Oberon is referring to Bottom

49   *upbraid her:* told her off; *fall out:* had a fight

Titania: What, wilt thou hear some music, my sweet love?
Bottom: I have a reasonable good ear in music. Let's have
    the tongs and the bones.
Titania: Or say, sweet love, what thou desirest to eat.   30
Bottom: Truly, a peck of provender: I could munch your
    good dry oats. Methinks I have a great desire to a bottle
    of hay: good hay, sweet hay, hath no fellow.
Titania: I have a venturous fairy that shall seek
    The squirrel's hoard, and fetch thee new nuts.   35
Bottom: I had rather have a handful or two of dried peas.
    But, I pray you, let none of your people stir me: I
    have an exposition of sleep come upon me.
Titania: Sleep thou, and I will wind thee in my arms.
    Fairies, be gone, and be all ways away.   40

                             [Exeunt Fairies.]

So doth the woodbine the sweet honeysuckle
Gently entwist; the female ivy so
Enrings the barky fingers of the elm.
O, how I love thee! how I dote on thee!

                             [They sleep.]

[Enter Puck.]

Oberon: [*Advancing*] Welcome, good Robin. See'st thou this
sweet sight?   45
    Her dotage now I do begin to pity:
    For, meeting her of late behind the wood,
    Seeking sweet favours for this hateful fool,
    I did upbraid her and fall out with her;
    For she his hairy temples then had rounded   50
    With coronet of fresh and fragrant flowers;
    And that same dew, which sometime on the buds
    Was wont to swell, like round and orient pearls,
    Stood now within the pretty flowerets' eyes
    Like tears that did their own disgrace bewail.   55
    When I had at my pleasure taunted her
    And she in mild terms begg'd my patience,
    I then did ask of her her changeling child;
    Which straight she gave me, and her fairy sent
    To bear him to my bower in fairy land.   60
    And now I have the boy, I will undo

65   *other:* the four lovers

66   *back again repair:* return

68   *fierce:* extravagant, wild

72   *Dian's bud o'er Cupid's flower:* Oberon is referring to the flower that is the antidote for the love potion.

80-81   *strike more . . . sense:* put the four lovers and Bottom into a sleep deeper than normal

85   *rock:* dance upon

86   *new in amity:* friends again

96   *compass:* encircle

This hateful imperfection of her eyes:
And, gentle Puck, take this transformèd scalp
From off the head of this Athenian swain;
That, he awaking when the other do,   65
May all to Athens back again repair
And think no more of this night's accidents
But as the fierce vexation of a dream.
But first I will release the fairy queen.
    Be as thou wast wont to be;   70
    See as thou wast wont to see:
    Dian's bud o'er Cupid's flower
    Hath such force and blessed power.
Now, my Titania; wake you, my sweet queen.
Titania: My Oberon! what visions have I seen!   75
    Methought I was enamour'd of an ass.
Oberon: There lies your love.
Titania: How came these things to pass?
    O, how mine eyes do loathe his visage now!
Oberon: Silence awhile. Robin, take off this head.
    Titania, music call; and strike more dead   80
    Than common sleep of all these five the sense.
Titania: Music, ho! music, such as charmeth sleep!
                             [*Music, still.*]
Puck: Now, when thou wakest, with thine own fool's eyes
    peep.
Oberon: Sound music! Come, my queen, take hands with
    me,
    And rock the ground whereon these sleepers be.   85
    Now thou and I are new in amity
    And will to-morrow midnight solemnly
    Dance in Duke Theseus' house triumphantly
    And bless it to all fair prosperity:
    There shall the pairs of faithful lovers be   90
    Wedded, with Theseus, all in jollity.
Puck: Fairy king, attend, and mark:
    I do hear the morning lark.
Oberon: Then, my queen, in silence sad,
    Trip we after night's shade: 95
    We the globe can compass soon,
    Swifter than the wandering moon.

102   *forester:* the gameskeeper

103   *observation:* the ritual celebration of May Day

104   *have the vaward:* are in the early part

106   *Uncouple:* unleash them

111   *Hercules, Cadmus:* other male heroes

112   *bay'd:* a hunting term meaning that the prey cannot escape and must turn and face the hounds

113   *hounds of Sparta:* a breed of hunting dog

114   *chiding:* barking

119   *flew'd:* large lower lips; *sanded:* sandy-coloured

121   *Thessalian:* Thessaly in northern Greece was famous for its bulls.

Titania: Come, my lord, and in our flight
          Tell me how it came this night,
          That I sleeping here was found   100
          With these mortals on the ground.

                                        [*Exeunt.*]
                              [*Horns winded within.*]

          [*Enter Theseus, Hippolyta, Egeus, and train.*]

Theseus: Go, one of you, find out the forester;
          For now our observation is perform'd;
          And since we have the vaward of the day,
          My love shall hear the music of my hounds.   105
          Uncouple in the western valley; let them go:
          Dispatch, I say, and find the forester.

                                  [*Exit an Attendant.*]
          We will, fair queen, up to the mountain's top
          And mark the musical confusion
          Of hounds and echo in conjunction.   110
Hippolyta: I was with Hercules and Cadmus once,
          When in a wood of Crete they bay'd the bear
          With hounds of Sparta: never did I hear
          Such gallant chiding; for, besides the groves,
          The skies, the fountains, every region near   115
          Seem'd all one mutual cry: I never heard
          So musical a discord, such sweet thunder.
Theseus: My hounds are bred out of the Spartan kind,
          So flew'd, so sanded, and their heads are hung
          With ears that sweep away the morning dew;   120
          Crook-knee'd, and dew-lapp'd like Thessalian bulls;
          Slow in pursuit, but match'd in mouth like bells,
          Each under each. A cry more tuneable
          Was never holla'd to, nor cheer'd with horn,
          In Crete, in Sparta, nor in Thessaly: 125
          Judge when you hear. But, soft! what nymphs are these?
Egeus: My lord, this is my daughter here asleep;
          And this, Lysander; this Demetrius is;
          This Helena, old Nedar's Helena:
          I wonder of their being here together.   130
Theseus: No doubt they rose up early to observe
          The rite of May, and, hearing our intent,

131

133   *in grace of our solemnity:* to honour our observance of the same rites

138-139 *Saint Valentine . . . now:* It was believed that birds chose their mates on St. Valentine's Day. (Theseus is joking at their expense.)

142   *concord:* agreement, harmony

143   *jealousy:* suspicion

163   *wot:* know

166   *idle gaud:* worthless trinket

Came here in grace of our solemnity.
But speak, Egeus; is not this the day
That Hermia should give answer of her choice?   135
Egeus: It is, my lord.
Theseus: Go, bid the huntsmen wake them with their
    horns.   [*Horns and shout within. Lysander, Demetrius,*
               Helena, and Hermia wake and start up.]
Good-morrow, friends. Saint Valentine is past:
Begin these wood-birds but to couple now?
Lysander: Pardon, my lord.
Theseus: I pray you all, stand up.   140
    I know you two are rival enemies:
    How comes this gentle concord in the world,
    That hatred is so far from jealousy,
    To sleep by hate, and fear no enmity?
Lysander: My lord, I shall reply amazedly,   145
    Half sleep, half waking; but as yet, I swear,
    I cannot truly say how I came here;
    But, as I think,—for truly would I speak,
    And now I do bethink me, so it is,—
    I came with Hermia hither: our intent   150
    Was to be gone from Athens, where we might,
    Without the peril of the Athenian law—
Egeus: Enough, enough, my lord; you have enough:
    I beg the law, the law, upon his head.
    They would have stolen away; they would, Demetrius,   155
    Thereby to have defeated you and me,
    You of your wife and me of my consent,
    Of my consent that she should be your wife.
Demetrius: My lord, fair Helen told me of their stealth,
    Of this their purpose hither to this wood;   160
    And I in fury hither follow'd them,
    Fair Helena in fancy following me.
    But, my good lord, I wot not by what power,—
    But by some power it is,—my love to Hermia,
    Melted as the snow, seems to me now   165
    As the remembrance of an idle gaud
    Which in my childhood I did dote upon;
    And all the faith, the virtue of my heart,
    The object and the pleasure of mine eye,

181   *for the morning . . . worn:* the morning's almost gone

188   *parted eye:* out of focus

190-191 *And I have found . . . own:* Demetrius is like some precious thing found by accident and is only mine until claimed by the owner

202   *God's my life:* a mild oath, probably meaning "God save me!"

204   *past the wit of man:* beyond man's understanding

Is only Helena. To her, my lord, 170
Was I betroth'd ere I saw Hermia:
But, like in sickness, did I loathe this food;
But, as in health, come to my natural taste,
Now I do wish it, love it, long for it,
And will for evermore be true to it. 175
Theseus: Fair lovers, you are fortunately met:
Of this discourse we more will hear anon.
Egeus, I will overbear your will;
For in the temple, by and by, with us
These couples shall eternally be knit: 180
And, for the morning now is something worn,
Our purposed hunting shall be set aside.
Away with us to Athens; three and three,
We'll hold a feast in great solemnity.
Come, Hippolyta. 185
    [*Exeunt Theseus, Hippolyta, Egeus, and train.*]
Demetrius: These things seem small and undistinguishable,
Like far-off mountains turned into clouds.
Hermia: Methinks I see these things with parted eye,
When every thing seems double.
Helena: So methinks:
And I have found Demetrius like a jewel, 190
Mine own, and not mine own.
Demetrius: Are you sure
That we are awake? It seems to me
That yet we sleep, we dream. Do not you think
The duke was here, and bid us follow him?
Hermia: Yea; and my father.
Helena: And Hippolyta. 195
Lysander: And he did bid us follow to the temple.
Demetrius: Why, then, we are awake: let's follow him; *how does H*
And by the way let us recount our dreams. *feel about D?*
        [*Exeunt.*]
Bottom: [*Awaking*] When my cue comes, call me, and I will
answer: my next is, "Most fair Pyramus." Heigh-ho! 200
Peter Quince! Flute, the bellows-mender! Snout, the
tinker! Starveling! God's my life, stolen hence, and
left me asleep! I have had a most rare vision. I have had
a dream, past the wit of man to say what dream it was:

205   *go about:* tries, attempts; *expound:* explain

208   *patched fool:* A court jester or king's fool wore clothes made up of materials of different colours and fabrics.

214   *hath no bottom:* meaning he can't get to the bottom of it; he can't understand it

215   *peradventure:* perhaps

216   *gracious:* attractive; *her:* Thisbe's

man is but an ass, if he go about to expound this dream. 205
Methought I was,—there is no man can tell what.
Methought I was,—and methought I had,—but man
is but a patched fool, if he will offer to say what
methought I had. The eye of man hath not heard, the
ear of man hath not seen, man's hand is not able to 210
taste, his tongue to conceive, nor his heart to report,
what my dream was. I will get Peter Quince to write a
ballad of this dream: it shall be called Bottom's Dream,
because it hath no bottom; and I will sing it in the latter
end of a play, before the duke: peradventure, to make 215
it the more gracious, I shall sing it at her death.

[Exit.]

Act 4, Scene 1: Activities

1. According to the stage directions, this scene continues from the last scene (Act 3, Scene 2) with no change of setting. As the director of this play, how would you handle the change from Act 3 to Act 4? Would you make some kind of change in the scenery? What signal would you use to show the break between the end of Act 3 and the beginning of Act 4?

2. Even though Titania has already given the servant-child to Oberon, he continues to watch her show her affection for Bottom while she is under the love-spell. Why does Oberon delay in removing the spell? What does his delay suggest about Oberon's character? When have you (or someone you know) continued to be the brunt of a joke when it wasn't funny anymore?

   In your journal explain how you feel about jokes that are played on others. When are the jokes not harmful to the person(s) on whom they are being played? When are they harmful to the person(s)?

3. Hippolyta and Theseus, who are about to be married, disagree on the qualities that are needed in dogs used for hunts (see lines 111-126). What qualities of the dogs does Hippolyta prefer? Which qualities does Theseus prefer? In your opinion how important is it for people who are planning to be married to share the same viewpoint?

   Talk about your ideas with a partner and share your observations with other partner groups.

4. When Demetrius admits that he must have been a sick man to stop loving Helena, and that he will love her forever, Helena responds by saying "Mine own and not mine own." (line 191). What do you think she means? Should she feel uncertain about Demetrius? Why or why not? Talk about your ideas in your group.

Do you think it's possible for one person to have complete power over another? Discuss your ideas with your group.

5. a) Bottom says that he wants Quince to write a ballad called "Bottom's Dream, because it hath no bottom." Recalling what has happened to Bottom since Puck placed the asshead on him, why do you think he suggests that his dream "hath no bottom"?

   Dreams usually don't make much sense in the real world. What kind of dream do you think would fit the definition of "having no bottom"?

   b) In groups write your own ballad called 'Bottom's Dream." You could put it to music and perform it for the class. Before you begin, examine other ballads to learn the ballad form.

6. When Bottom wakes from his dream he says that only a fool would attempt to explain to him what happened.

   How do you think Bottom feels? Consider the following questions:
   • Is he fearful of his dream? If so, how does he reveal his fear?
   • Does he reject the dream as impossible? If so, how does he explain the fact that he actually had the dream?

   In your groups talk about your response to these two questions. Report your conclusions to other groups.

For the next scene . . .

Recall a time when someone was *very* late to pick you up. How did you feel while you were waiting? What went through your mind? What did you decide to do? How did you handle the situation when he or she finally arrived?

Act 4, Scene 2

In this scene . . .

Back in Athens, Bottom's friends (who are at Peter Quince's house) are worried because Bottom hasn't yet returned from the woods. Suddenly Bottom arrives just in time for the rehearsal to continue. He urges his friends to hurry to the palace for their performance, saying that he can't explain his mysterious disappearance. He reassures his friends that later he will tell them "everything, right as it fell out."

4   *transported:* carried away by the fairies

5   *marred:* ruined

8   *discharge:* perform

9   *best wit:* best ability (to perform)

12   *paramour:* a lover, usually in an immoral way

13   *paragon:* a model (perfect) person

14   *a thing of naught:* something wicked

17-18   *we had all . . . men:* made our fortunes

19-20   *sixpence a day:* his royal pension

20-21   *he could not . . . day:* his reward would certainly not have been less

24   *hearts:* good fellows

Scene 2

Athens. Quince's house.

*Enter Quince, Flute, Snout, and
Starveling.*

Quince: Have you sent to Bottom's house? is he come home
    yet?
Starveling: He cannot be heard of. Out of doubt he is
    transported.
Flute: If he come not, then the play is marred: it goes not   5
    forward, doth it?
Quince: It is not possible: you have not a man in all Athens
    able to discharge Pyramus but he.
Flute: No, he hath simply the best wit of any handicraft
    man in Athens.   10
Quince: Yea, and the best person too; and he is a very
    paramour for a sweet voice.
Flute: You must say "paragon": a paramour is, God bless
    us, a thing of naught.

   [*Enter Snug.*]

Snug: Masters, the Duke is coming from the temple, and   15
    there is two or three lords and ladies more married: if
    our sport had gone forward, we had all been made
    men.
Flute: O sweet Bully Bottom! Thus hath he lost sixpence a
    day during his life; he could not have 'scaped sixpence   20
    a day: an the duke had not given him sixpence a day for
    playing Pyramus, I'll be hanged; he would have
    deserved it: sixpence a day in Pyramus, or nothing.

   [*Enter Bottom.*]

Bottom: Where are these lads? where are these hearts?
Quince: Bottom! O most courageous day! O most happy   25
    hour!

29   *right as it fell out:* exactly as it happened

32-33   *good strings to your beards:* new strings to tie the false beards
        on with

33   *new ribbons to your pumps:* new laces for their shoes

35   *preferred:* recommended

Bottom: Masters, I am to discourse wonders: but ask me
    not what; for if I tell you, I am no true Athenian. I will
    tell you everything, right as it fell out.
Quince: Let us hear, sweet Bottom.   30
Bottom: Not a word of me. All that I will tell you is, that
    the Duke hath dined. Get your apparel together, good
    strings to your beards, ncw ribbons to your pumps;
    meet presently at the palace; every man look o'er his
    part; for the short and the long is, our play is preferred.   35
    In any case, let Thisby have clean linen; and let not
    him that plays the lion pare his nails, for they shall hang
    out for the lion's claws. And, most dear actors, eat no
    onions nor garlic, for we are to utter sweet breath; and
    I do not doubt but to hear them say, it is a sweet   40
    comedy. No more words: away! go, away!   [*Exeunt.*]

Act 4, Scene 2: Activities

1. If Bottom doesn't arrive at Quince's house, the rest of the players think they won't be able to present their play.

   Why do they feel only Bottom can play the role of the mythical lover Pyramus? What acting abilities do they praise in Bottom?

   If you were Quince and thought Bottom might not arrive in time for the performance, what solution(s) would you consider other than cancelling the show?

2. As a group activity, rewrite this short scene in modern dialogue and present it to the class.

3. a) Flute and Quince (in particular) seem upset about Bottom's disappearance. Is there any difference in the way they express their feelings? As a director what suggestions would you make to the actors playing these roles?

   Would you have each actor use a different tone of voice from the other one?

   Would you have one of them show anger? Which one would show sadness and disappointment in his tone of voice?

   Select two people to play the roles of Flute and Quince in lines 1-14 and have them perform the lines for an audience. Have the audience comment on the effec-tiveness of the way both actors play the different characters.

   b) As Quince, would you want an explanation from Bottom for his late arrival? Write what you as Quince would say to Bottom when he finally showed up at your house.

   With a partner, deliver your speech to the person playing Bottom. Have your partner deliver Bottom's response.

Act 4: Consider the Whole Act

1. Bottom ends Act 4 saying "No more words: away! go, away!" (line 41). Do you think the play coud end here? Has everything been settled to your satisfaction? Do you think there are things that still need to be cleared up? In two columns, record the reasons why you believe the play should end or should not end at this point. You might wish to form two teams and debate the issue.

2. Because Bottom, Titania and the four lovers are all put to sleep at the end of their adventures in the wood, they assume their adventures were really dreams.

   Reread the sections where Titania, the lovers and Bottom wake up. Describe how each character interprets what happened to him or her. What did each character gain from the adventure?

   If you could be one of the "dreamers," who would you choose to be? Write a paper explaining your choice.

3. In groups, select a part of a scene from Act 4 that you would like to prepare for a video-short. Decide what moments in the action you would like to highlight and select people to deliver the lines for the characters involved.

   Practise with the camera to get a "feel" for it before you start shooting the segment. Share your video with the rest of the class.

For the next scene . . .

Have you ever been in a situation where you told someone about something strange that had happened to you, and the person thought you were making the whole story up? How did you feel? In your journal, record what you wished you had said to the disbeliever.

Act 5, Scene 1

In this scene . . .

Back at Theseus' palace, the three marriages have already taken place. Hippolyta now becomes interested in the story that the lovers have told. Theseus, however, dismisses the whole tale as imagined nonsense. The three couples then discuss the entertainment that is being offered to them by the citizens of Athens. Theseus chooses to have Bottom's group perform "Pyramus and Thisbe." When the play is over, everyone retires to bed. The fairies enter the palace, and Oberon has his attendants bless everyone in the house. He himself blesses the royal union.

1   *that:* what

2   *may:* can

3   *antique:* strange

4   *seething:* excitable

5   *shaping fantasies:* an ability to create or invent;
     apprehend: perceive, imagine

6   *ever comprehends:* can ever understand

8   *all compact:* formed, composed

11   *Helen's beauty:* reference to Helen of Troy, a woman whose
     beauty was the cause of the Trojan War; a *brow of Egypt:* a term
     meaning a gypsy

14   *bodies forth:* invents, creates

16   *them:* that is, the new invention or creations

16-17 *gives to airy . . . name:* and gives this newly invented thing a
     name and shape

20   *comprehends . . . joy:* has no trouble creating in his imagination
     some source of the joy

24   *transfigured:* changed

25   *More witnesseth . . . images:* gives evidence of more than just
     the imagination inventing things

26   *grows to:* arrives at; *constancy:* consistency, certainty

Act 5, Scene 1

Athens. The palace of Theseus.

*Enter Theseus, Hippolyta,
Philostrate, Lords, and Attendants.*

Hippolyta: 'Tis strange, my Theseus, that these lovers speak
    of.
Theseus: More strange than true: I never may believe
   These antique fables, nor these fairy toys.
   Lovers and madmen have such seething brains,
   Such shaping fantasies, that apprehend   5
   More than cool reason ever comprehends.
   The lunatic, the lover, and the poet
   Are of imagination all compact:
   One sees more devils than vast hell can hold,
   That is, the madman: the lover, all as frantic,   10
   Sees Helen's beauty in a brow of Egypt:
   The poet's eye, in a fine frenzy rolling,
   Doth glance from heaven to earth, from earth to heaven,
   And as imagination bodies forth
   The forms of things unknown, the poet's pen   15
   Turns them to shapes and gives to airy nothing
   A local habitation and a name.
   Such tricks hath strong imagination,
   That, if it would but apprehend some joy,
   It comprehends some bringer of that joy;   20
   Or in the night, imagining some fear,
   How easy is a bush supposed a bear!
Hippolyta: But all the story of the night told over,
   And all their minds transfigured so together,
   More witnesseth than fancy's images,   25
   And grows to something of great constancy;
   But, howsoever, strange and admirable.
Theseus: Here come the lovers, full of joy and mirth.

32   *masque:* a spectacle in which costumes, scenery, music, and dancing are of great importance, a form of entertainment popular in 16th and 17th century England

39   *abridgement:* pastime (to shorten the time)

42   *brief:* list; *ripe:* ready

44-47   *The battle . . . Hercules:* a battle in which Theseus and his kinsman Hercules successfully fought the centaurs (creatures half-horse, half man). The battle took place during a wedding, and Theseus has promised Hippolyta not to choose an entertainment with sad reminders.

48-51   *The riot . . . conqueror:* Theseus says this story of Orpheus being killed by the worshippers of Bacchus is an old play.

52   *thrice three Muses:* the nine goddesses of the arts

55   *sorting with:* fitting to, suited to

60   *concord:* agreement, harmony

[*Enter Lysander, Demetrius, Hermia, and Helena.*]

Joy, gentle friends! joy and fresh days of love
Accompany your hearts!

Lysander: More than to us   30
Wait in your royal walks, your board, your bed!

Theseus: Come now; what masques, what dances shall we
    have,
To wear away this long age of three hours
Between our after-supper and bed-time?
Where is our usual manager of mirth?   35
What revels are in hand? Is there no play,
To ease the anguish of a torturing hour?
Call Philostrate.

Philostrate: Here, mighty Theseus.

Theseus: Say, what abridgement have you for this evening?
What masque? what music? How shall we beguile   40
The lazy time, if not with some delight?

Philostrate: There is a brief how many sports are ripe:
Make choice of which your highness will see first.
                    [*Giving a paper.*]

Theseus: [*Reads*] "The battle with the Centaurs, to be sung
By an Athenian eunuch to the harp."   45
We'll none of that: that have I told my love,
In glory of my kinsman Hercules.
[*Reads.*] "The riot of the tipsy Bacchanals,
Tearing the Thracian singer in their rage."
That is an old device; and it was play'd   50
When I from Thebes came last a conqueror.
[*Reads*] "The thrice three Muses mourning for the death
Of Learning, late deceased in beggary."
That is some satire, keen and critical,
Not sorting with a nuptial ceremony.   55
[*Reads*] "A tedious brief scene of young Pyramus
And his love Thisbe; very tragical mirth."
Merry and tragical! tedious and brief!
That is, hot ice and wondrous strange snow.
How shall we find the concord of this discord?   60

Philostrate: A play there is, my lord, some ten words long,
Which is as brief as I have known a play;

65   *fitted:* suited to the part

74   *toil'd:* taxed, strained; *unbreathed:* unexercised

75   *against:* in preparation for

79-81 *Unless you . . . service:* unless you can find amusement in their extremely strained attempts to learn their lines in your honour

83   *simpleness:* sincerity

85   *wretchedness o'ercharged:* poor people trying to do what is beyond them

86   *duty . . . perishing:* being ruined or disgraced

88   *can do . . . kind:* cannot act

90   *Our sport . . . mistake:* our entertainment will be to accept politely the mistakes they make

91-92 *And what . . . merit:* a noble person respects the intention even when the performance is inadequate

93   *Where I have come:* places where I've been; *clerks:* scholars

94   *premeditated:* carefully prepared

97   *Throttle . . . fears:* stutter and choke over carefully prepared speeches because of nervousness

But by ten words, my lord, it is too long,
Which makes it tedious; for in all the play
There is not one word apt, one player fitted: 65
And tragical, my noble lord, it is;
For Pyramus therein doth kill himself.
Which, when I saw rehearsed, I must confess,
Made mine eyes water; but more merry tears
The passion of loud laughter never shed.   70
Theseus: What are they that do play it?
Philostrate: Hard-handed men, that work in Athens here,
Which never labour'd in their minds till now,
And now have toil'd their unbreathed memories
With this same play, against your nuptial.   75
Theseus: And we will hear it.
Philostrate: No, my noble lord;
It is not for you: I have heard it over,
And it is nothing, nothing in the world;
Unless you can find sport in their intents,
Extremely stretch'd and conn'd with cruel pain,   80
To do you service.
Theseus: I will hear that play;
For never anything can be amiss,
When simpleness and duty tender it.
Go, bring them in: and take your places, ladies.
                                        [*Exit Philostrate.*]
Hippolyta: I love not to see wretchedness o'ercharged,   85
And duty in his service perishing.
Theseus: Why, gentle sweet, you shall see no such thing.
Hippolyta: He says they can do nothing in this kind.
Theseus: The kinder we, to give them thanks for nothing.
Our sport shall be to take what they mistake: 90
And what poor duty cannot do, noble respect
Takes it in might, not merit.
Where I have come, great clerks have purposed
To greet me with premeditated welcomes;
Where I have seen them shiver and look pale,   95
Make periods in the midst of sentences,
Throttle their practised accent in their fears
And in conclusion dumbly have broke off,
Not paying me a welcome. Trust me, sweet,

102   *I read as much as from:* I got as much out of

104   *tongue-tied simplicity:* nervous sincerity

105   *In least speak most:* says more; *to my capacity:* in my opinion

106   *address'd:* ready

118   *stand upon points:* use proper punctuation. (The speech in lines 108-117 is not properly punctuated because of Quince's nervousness.)

123   *recorder:* a type of flute; *not in government:* not with control

Out of this silence yet I pick'd a welcome;   100
And in the modesty of fearful duty
I read as much as from the rattling tongue
Of saucy and audacious eloquence.
Love, therefore, and tongue-tied simplicity
In least speak most, to my capacity.   105

[*Re-enter Philostrate.*]

Philostrate: So please your grace, the Prologue is address'd.
Theseus: Let him approach.   [*Flourish of trumpets.*]

[*Enter Quince for the Prologue.*]

Prologue:
  If we offend, it is with our good will.
    That you should think, we come not to offend,
  But with good will. To show our simple skill,   110
    That is the true beginning of our end.
  Consider then we come but in despite.
    We do not come as minding to content you,
  Our true intent is. All for your delight
    We are not here. That you should here repent you,   115
  The actors are at hand and by their show
  You shall know all that you are like to know.
Theseus: This fellow doth not stand upon points.
Lysander: He hath rid his prologue like a rough colt; he
    knows not the stop. A good moral, my lord: it is not   120
    enough to speak, but to speak true.
Hippolyta: Indeed he hath played on his prologue like a child
    on a recorder; a sound, but not in government.
Theseus: His speech was like a tangled chain; nothing
    impaired, but all disordered. Who is next?   125

[*Enter Pyramus and Thisbe, Wall, Moonshine, and Lion.*]

Prologue:
  Gentles, perchance you wonder at this show;
    But wonder on, till truth make all things plain.
  This man is Pyramus, if you would know;
    This beauteous lady Thisby is certain.
  This man, with lime and rough-cast, doth present   130
    Wall, that vile Wall which did these lovers sunder;

138   *hight:* is called

162   *right and sinister:* running right and left – a horizontal crack

And through Wall's chink, poor souls, they are content
   To whisper. At the which let no man wonder.
This man, with lanthorn, dog, and bush of thorn,
   Presenteth Moonshine; for, if you will know,   135
By moonshine did these lovers think no scorn
   To meet at Ninus' tomb, there, there to woo.
This grisly beast, which Lion hight by name,
   The trusty Thisby, coming first by night,
Did scare away, or rather did affright;   140
   And, as she fled, her mantle she did fall,
Which Lion vile with bloody mouth did stain.
   Anon comes Pyramus, sweet youth and tall,
And finds his trusty Thisby's mantle slain:
   Whereat, with blade, with bloody blameful blade,   145
He bravely broach'd his boiling bloody breast;
   And Thisby, tarrying in mulberry shade,
His dagger drew, and died. For all the rest,
   Let Lion, Moonshine, Wall, and lovers twain
At large discourse, while here they do remain.   150
               [Exeunt Prologue, Pyramus, Thisbe, Lion, and
                                    Moonshine.]

Theseus: I wonder if the lion be to speak.
Demetrius: No wonder, my lord: one lion may, when many
   asses do.
Wall: In this same interlude it doth befall
That I, one Snout by name, present a wall;   155
And such a wall, as I would have you think,
That had in it a crannied hole or chink,
Through which the lovers, Pyramus and Thisby,
Did whisper often very secretly.
This loam, this rough-cast and this stone doth show   160
That I am that same wall; the truth is so:
And this the cranny is, right and sinister,
Through which the fearful lovers are to whisper.
Theseus: Would you desire lime and hair to speak better?
Demetrius: It is the wittiest partition that ever I heard   165
   discourse, my lord.
Theseus: Pyramus draws near the wall: silence!

  [Re-enter Pyramus.]

Pyramus: O grim-look'd night! O night with hue so black!

184   *fall pat:* happen exactly

190-191 *I see . . . face:* Bottom changes the functions of the senses as he did when talking about his dream (Act 4, Scene 1, lines 213-215).

195-196 *Limander and Helen:* blunders for Leander and Hero, another pair of famous lovers

197   *Shafalus and Procrus:* blunders for Cephalus and Procris, a famous married couple

202   *'Tide life,' tide death:* come life or death

O night, which ever art when day is not!
O night, O night! alack, alack, alack, 170
   I fear my Thisby's promise is forgot!
And thou, O wall, O sweet, O lovely wall,
   That stand'st between her father's ground and mine!
Thou wall, O wall, O sweet and lovely wall,
   Show me thy chink, to blink through with mine eyne! 175
                      [Wall holds up his fingers.]
Thanks, courteous wall: Jove shield thee well for this!
   But what see I? No Thisby do I see.
O wicked wall, through whom I see no bliss!
   Cursed be thy stones for thus deceiving me!
Theseus: The wall, methinks, being sensible, should curse 180
   again.
Pyramus: No, in truth, sir, he should not. "Deceiving me"
   is Thisby's cue: she is to enter now, and I am to spy
   her through the wall. You shall see, it will fall pat as I
   told you. Yonder she comes. 185

[Re-enter Thisbe.]

Thisbe: O wall, full often hast thou heard my moans,
   For parting my fair Pyramus and me!
My cherry lips have often kiss'd thy stones,
   Thy stones with lime and hair knit up in thee.
Pyramus: I see a voice: now will I to the chink, 190
   To spy an I can hear my Thisby's face.
   Thisby!
Thisbe: My love thou art, my love I think.
Pyramus: Think what thou wilt, I am thy lover's grace
   And, like Limander, am I trusty still. 195
Thisbe: And I like Helen, till the Fates me kill.
Pyramus: Not Shafalus to Procrus was so true.
Thisbe: As Shafalus to Procrus, I to you.
Pyramus: O kiss me through the hole of this vile wall!
Thisbe: I kiss the wall's hole, not your lips at all. 200
Pyramus: Wilt thou at Ninny's tomb meet me straightway?
Thisbe: 'Tide life, 'tide death, I come without delay.
               [Exeunt Pyramus and Thisbe.]
Wall: Thus have I, Wall, my part discharged so;
   And being done, thus Wall away doth go. *[Exit.]*

205   *mural:* wall

210-211 *The best . . . amend them:* The best actors would only have
         something to suggest or represent (shadow) things like walls.
         We have to use our imagination with a play like this one.

221   *lion-fell:* fierce lion. This term may also mean lion-skin and would
         then be an unintentional joke about his costume; *dam:* mother

234   *horned moon:* the new moon or crescent moon with its two points

236   *He is no crescent:* a joke about Moonshine's weight – he isn't
         a thin man, like the new (thin) moon

Theseus: Now is the mural down between the two   205
  neighbours.
Demetrius: No remedy, my lord, when walls are so wilful
  to hear without warning.
Hippolyta: This is the silliest stuff that ever I heard.
Theseus: The best in this kind are but shadows; and the   210
  worst are no worse, if imagination amend them.
Hippolyta: It must be your imagination then, and not theirs.
Theseus: If we imagine no worse of them than they of
  themselves, they may pass for excellent men. Here come
  two noble beasts in, a man and a lion.   215

[*Re-enter Lion and Moonshine.*]

Lion: You, ladies, you, whose gentle hearts do fear
  The smallest monstrous mouse that creeps on floor,
May now perchance both quake and tremble here,
  When lion rough in wildest rage doth roar.
Then know that I, one Snug the joiner, am   220
  A lion-fell, nor else no lion's dam;
For, if I should as lion come in strife
  Into this place, 'twere pity on my life.
Theseus: A very gentle beast, and of a good conscience.
Demetrius: The very best at a beast, my lord, that e'er I   225
  saw.
Lysander: This lion is a very fox for his valour.
Theseus: True; and a goose for his discretion.
Demetrius: Not so, my lord; for his valour cannot carry his
discretion; and the fox carries the goose.   230
Theseus: His discretion, I am sure, cannot carry his valour;
  for the goose carries not the fox. It is well; leave it to
  his discretion, and let us listen to the moon.
Moonshine: This lanthorn doth the horned moon present;—
Demetrius: He should have worn the horns on his head.   235
Theseus: He is no crescent, and his horns are invisible within
  the circumference.
Moonshine: This lanthorn doth the horned moon present;—
  Myself the man i' the moon do seem to be.
Theseus: This is the greatest error of all the rest: the man   240
  should be put into the lanthorn. How is it else the
  man i' the moon?

244   *in snuff:* a pun on a candle being snuffed out and a person being angry

248   *in the wane:* his speech or part is almost over

263   *moused:* shaken, torn (like a mouse in the jaws of a cat)

266   *sunny beams:* another of Bottom's typical blunders. "Sunny beams" describes sunlight, not moonlight.

272   *dole:* grievous sight

Demetrius: He dares not come there for the candle; for you see, it is already in snuff.

Hippolyta: I am aweary of this moon: would he would   245
change!

Theseus: It appears, by his small light of discretion, that he is in the wane; but yet, in courtesy, in all reason, we must stay the time.

Lysander: Proceed, Moon.   250

Moonshine: All that I have to say, is, to tell you that the lanthorn is the moon; I, the man in the moon; this thorn-bush, my thorn-bush; and this dog, my dog.

Demetrius: Why, all these should be in the lanthorn; for all these are in the moon. But, silence! here comes   255
Thisbe.

[*Re-enter Thisbe.*]

Thisbe: This is old Ninny's tomb. Where is my love?

Lion: [*Roaring*] Oh——   [*Thisbe runs off.*]

Demetrius: Well roared, Lion.

Theseus: Well run, Thisbe.   260

Hippolyta: Well shone, Moon. Truly, the moon shines with a good grace.

          [*The Lion shakes Thisbe's mantle, and exit.*]

Theseus: Well moused, Lion.

Lysander: And so the lion vanished.

Demetrius: And then came Pyramus.   265

[*Re-enter Pyramus.*]

Pyramus: Sweet Moon, I thank thee for thy sunny beams;
    I thank thee, Moon, for shining now so bright;
For, by thy gracious, golden, glittering gleams,
    I trust to take of truest Thisby sight.
              But stay, O spite!   270
              But mark, poor knight,
        What dreadful dole is here!
            Eyes, do you see?
            How can it be?
        O dainty duck! O dear!   275
            Thy mantle good,
        What, stain'd with blood!

278   *Furies:* the three goddesses of vengeance

280   *thread and thrum:* a term used in weaving – *thrum* is the fluffy
       end of the threads. Bottom calls upon Atropos, one of the three
       goddesses of Fate, to cut the thread (line) of human life.

284   *Beshrew my heart:* a mild curse meaning "May evil befall me."

285   *frame:* create

291   *pap:* breast or heart

298-299 *Tongue . . . flight:* Bottom mixes up his lines. He should have
         said "Tongue take your flight" meaning be made dumb (dead),
         and "Moon lose thy light," meaning the Moon's light goes out
         for Pyramus, now dead. Instead, Moonshine walks off the
         stage.

301-305 *No die . . . an ass:* a series of puns on die (death) and die (for
         gambling), and on ace for one (one spot on the die; one actor
         left on stage) and on the similar sound of ace and ass

> Approach, ye Furies fell!
>> O Fates, come, come,
>>> Cut thread and thrum; 280
>> Quail, crush, conclude, and quell!

Theseus: This passion, and the death of a dear friend, would
go near to make a man look sad.

Hippolyta: Beshrew my heart, but I pity the man.

Pyramus: O wherefore, Nature, didst thou lions frame? 285
Since lion vile hath here deflower'd my dear:
Which is—no, no—which was the fairest dame
That lived, that loved, that liked, that look'd
with cheer.
>> Come, tears, confound;
>> Out, sword and wound 290
>> The pap of Pyramus;
>>> Ay, that left pap,
>>> Where heart doth hop:

[Stabs himself.]

>> Thus die I, thus, thus, thus.
>> Now am I dead 295
>> Now am I fled;
> My soul is in the sky:
>> Tongue, lose thy light:
>> Moon, take thy flight;

[Exit Moonshine.]

>> Now, die, die, die, die, die. 300

Demetrius: No die, but an ace, for him; for he is but one.

Lysander: Less than an ace, man; for he is dead; he is
nothing.

Theseus: With the help of a surgeon he might yet recover,
and prove an ass. 305

Hippolyta: How chance Moonshine is gone before Thisbe
comes back and finds her lover?

Theseus: She will find him by starlight. Here she comes;
and her passion ends the play.

[*Re-enter Thisbe.*]

Hippolyta: Methinks she should not use a long one for such 310
a Pyramus: I hope she will be brief.

Demetrius: A mote will turn the balance, which

316   *videlicet:* that is to say

329   *Sisters Three:* the three Fates

333   *shore:* cut (shorn)
334   *thread of silk:* thread of life

337   *imbue:* stain with blood

344-345 *see* and *hear:* confused by Bottom; *Bergomask:* a dance from
        Bergamo, Italy

Pyramus, which Thisbe, is the better; he for a man,
God warrant us; she for a woman, God bless us.
Lysander: She hath spied him already with those sweet eyes.   315
Demetrius: And thus she means, videlicet;—
Thisbe: Asleep, my love?
                What, dead, my dove?
            O Pyramus, arise!
                Speak, speak. Quite dumb?   320
                Dead, dead? A tomb
            Must cover thy sweet eyes.
                These lily lips,
                This cherry nose,
            These yellow cowslip cheeks,   325
                Are gone, are gone;
                Lovers, make moan:
            His eyes were green as leeks.
                O Sisters Three,
                Come, come to me,   330
            With hands as pale as milk;
                Lay them in gore,
                Since you have shore
            With shears his thread of silk.
                Tongue, not a word: 335
                Come, trusty sword;
            Come, blade, my breast imbue:
                                    [*Stabs herself.*]
                And, farewell friends;
                Thus Thisby ends:
            Adieu, adieu, adieu.   [*Dies.*] 340
Theseus: Moonshine and Lion are left to bury the dead.
Demetrius: Ay, and Wall too.
Bottom: [*Starting up*] No, I assure you; the wall is down
    that parted their fathers. Will it please you to see the
epilogue, or to hear a Bergomask dance between two   345
    of our company?
Theseus: No epilogue, I pray you; for your play needs no
    excuse. Never excuse; for when the players are all dead,
    there need none to be blamed. Marry, if he that writ
    it had played Pyramus and hanged himself in Thisbe's 350
    garter, it would have been a fine tragedy: and so it is,

354   *The iron . . . twelve:* the clock has struck midnight

357   *overwatch'd:* stayed up too late
358   *palpable-gross:* obviously dull or crude

365   *fordone:* exhausted
366   *wasted . . . glow:* the logs have burned down to embers

372   *sprite:* spirit or ghost

375   *triple Hecate's team:* Hecate ruled in three capacities: as Luna in Heaven, Diana on earth, and Hecate in Hades. "Team" refers to her chariot.

378   *frolic:* merry

380-381 *I am sent . . . door:* Robin Goodfellow was a household spirit and often pictured holding a broom. Here he's been sent to clean the threshold for Oberon and Titania.

truly; and very notably discharged. But, come, your
Bergomask: let your epilogue alone.
[*A dance.*]
    The iron tongue of midnight hath told twelve:
    Lovers, to bed; 'tis almost fairy time.   355
    I fear we shall out-sleep the coming morn
    As much as we this night have overwatch'd.
    This palpable-gross play hath well beguiled
    The heavy gait of night. Sweet friends, to bed.
    A fortnight hold we this solemnity,   360
    In nightly revels and new jollity.   [*Exeunt.*]

  [*Enter Puck.*]

Puck: Now the hungry lion roars,
      And the wolf behowls the moon,
    Whilst the heavy ploughman snores,
      All with weary task fordone.   365
    Now the wasted brands do glow,
      Whilst the screech-owl, screeching loud,
    Puts the wretch that lies in woe
      In remembrance of a shroud.
    Now it is the time of night   370
      That the graves, all gaping wide,
    Every one lets forth his sprite,
      In the church-way paths to glide:
    And we fairies, that do run
      By the triple Hecate's team,   375
    From the presence of the sun,
      Following darkness like a dream,
    Now are frolic: not a mouse
    Shall disturb this hallow'd house:
    I am sent with broom before,   380
    To sweep the dust behind the door.

  [*Enter Oberon and Titania with their train.*]

Oberon: Through the house give glimmering light,
      By the dead and drowsy fire:
    Every elf and fairy sprite
      Hop as light as bird from brier;   385
    And this ditty, after me,

388   *by rote:* from memory

396   *issue:* children

403   *prodigious:* abnormal

404   *in nativity:* at birth

406   *consecrate:* bless, make sacred

407   *take his gait:* go your way

414   *shadows:* spirits

416   *but slumber'd here:* been asleep during the play (that is, Shakespeare's play, not Bottom's)

418   *this weak and idle theme:* the story in the play

419   *No more . . . dream:* was something you dreamed

420   *reprehend:* find fault with us

421   *mend:* do better next time

423   *unearned:* undeserved

Sing and dance it trippingly.
Titania: First, rehearse your song by rote,
    To each word a warbling note:
    Hand in hand, with fairy grace,   390
    Will we sing, and bless this place.

                                  [*Song and dance.*]

Oberon: Now, until the break of day,
    Through this house each fairy stray.
    To the best bride-bed will we,
    Which by us shall blessed be;   395
    And the issue there create
    Ever shall be fortunate.
    So shall all the couples three
    Ever true in loving be;
    And the blots of Nature's hand   400
    Shall not in their issue stand;
    Never mole, harc-lip, nor scar,
    Nor mark prodigious, such as are
    Despised in nativity,
    Shall upon their children be.   405
    With this field-dew consecrate,
    Every fairy take his gait;
    And each several chamber bless,
    Through this palace, with sweet peace;
    And the owner of it blest   410
    Ever shall in safety rest.
    Trip away! make no stay;
    Meet me all by break of day.

                    [*Exeunt Oberon, Titania, and train.*]

Puck:

    If we shadows have offended,
    Think but this and all is mended,   415
    That you have but slumber'd here
    While these visions did appear.
    And this weak and idle theme,
    No more yielding but a dream,
    Gentles, do not reprehend: 420
    If you pardon, we will mend:
    And, as I am an honest Puck,
    If we have unearned luck

424   *serpent's tongue:* hissing of the audience

428   *Give me your hands:* applaud me

429   *And Robin shall restore amends:* This is the third time (see lines 421 and 425) in which Puck promises something better in the future. Many critics have suggested that this is Shakespeare promising to return in a later play to the ideas he worked with in this play.

Now to 'scape the serpent's tongue,
We will make amends ere long;   425
Else the Puck a liar call:
So, good-night unto you all.
Give me your hands, if we be friends,
And Robin shall restore amends.   [*Exit.*]

Act 5, Scene 1: Activities

1. You are a gossip columnist for a local newspaper who attended the three wedding ceremonies at Theseus' palace. Write your column describing the festivities. You could include details such as the following:
   - descriptions of the brides' outfits.
   - comments Theseus made to you when you arrived at the palace.
   - the list of people who attended.
   - who was not invited to the celebration.

   You might wish to study the style that different gossip columnists use in their columns for newspapers and/or magazines before you begin.

2. If Shakespeare had written a scene between Egeus and Hermia in this act, what do you think the two would have said to each other? Do you think Egeus would have finally accepted his daughter's decision to marry Lysander?

   Write the scene as you think it would have occurred, and decide where you would insert it in the act.

   Present the dialogue to your group and be prepared to explain your reasons for writing what you did.

3. A composer named Felix Mendelssohn wrote music for *A Midsummer Night's Dream* in the eighteen hundreds. The music for Oberon's blessing of the marriages has become well-known. Find a copy of the record in your school or local library and play it to your group. You might dim the lights to create the evening celebration effect.

   Discuss the mood of this music and record your feelings in your journal.

4. At the beginning of the scene, Theseus says that he doesn't put much trust in the imaginations of lovers, madmen, or poets. He thinks that their brains grasp more

than reason can understand and that when they are frightened, they can mistake a bush for a bear.

Recall a lover, "mad" person, or poet you know or know about. Do you think his or her imagination is "more strange than true"?

In your journal, compare your own imagination to this person's, explaining whether you believe there really is a difference in the way people's imaginations work.

In what situation do you think you might "mistake a bush for a bear" or imagine that something totally harmless is really some dreadful monster about to attack you? Write about a possible situation that could drive your imagination out of the realm of the reasonable into a state of pure fantasy.

5. You are an inventor who has a brilliant idea for a new kitchen appliance. You need money to assist you in the research and development of your idea. Theseus is in a position to make some money available to you. Knowing what you do about his mistrust of the imagination, what argument would you use to win his faith in you and your idea? Write a letter to him, persuading him to grant you money to finance your remarkable invention.

6. Hippolyta is struck by the fact that the minds of the different lovers were affected in similar ways and that the details of their stories were much the same even though the stories were very strange. This leads her to believe that their stories are more than just fanciful imaginings.

Think of a dream you experienced or know that included real-life details. How did the real details make you feel about the dream? What explanation could you give to the addition of real-life moments in a "dream" state-of-mind?

In your journal, write your ideas about the relationship between dreams and reality.

7. Knowing what Theseus says about the story the four lovers tell (lines 2-22), what do you think he'd say to Bottom if he knew that Bottom wanted to write a book about his vision?

Imagine that Bottom has asked Theseus for time off work to write his book. With a partner, write the conversation that takes place between them. What arguments would Bottom use? How would Theseus respond? Record your dialogue and present it to your group.

8. You are an entertainment reporter for a television station. You have just returned from seeing "Pyramus and Thisbe." Write a review of the performance including your opinion about the quality of acting, the effectiveness of the props, and the comments to and from the audience. You might wish to include comments from actors and/or members of the audience made after the performance in interviews you conducted.

9. After the other characters have left, Puck creeps into the palace and describes the night — the wild animals that roar, howl, and screech and the ghosts that leave their graves to wander abroad.

In a group, plan a presentation of Puck's speech. Before you perform the speech, consider the following:
- Will you present a modern version of his speech or a Shakespearean version?
- Will you use background music? If so, what music would be appropriate?
- Will you have Puck present the speech alone or will you have a chorus of spirits and ghosts performing with him?
- What actions will Puck use to help him communicate his message?

When you are ready to perform the speech, present it live or prepare a video of it to show to other groups.

10. In groups, discuss whether or not you think it is appropriate for the play to end with a speech given by a mythical character, Puck, rather than ending the same way as it began, with a speech given by Theseus.

Consider the Whole Play

1. *A Midsummer Night's Dream* is often presented as a children's play partly because of its enchanted forest.

   Do you think this play is appropriate entertainment for children or do you think parts of it might be too difficult for children to understand?

   In your group, make a list of both the pros and cons of presenting the play to children. You might choose to debate the issue with members of your group or another group.

2. Find out as much as you can about the beliefs and festivities surrounding ceremonies of midsummer held in England and parts of Europe in the sixteen hundreds. In what ways does this information help you understand and interpret the play? Present your findings and observations to your group in a written or oral report. Encourage questions and discussion from your audience.

3. What do you think a marriage counsellor might say about the marriage of Theseus and Hippolyta? Remember that Hippolyta was Queen of the Amazons before she married.

   Before you prepare your response, you might want to do some research on the Amazons.

   Reread the sections of the play where Theseus and Hippolyta talk together. Present your thoughts in a letter beginning, "Dear . . . Theseus and Hippolyta."

4. Make a list of all the questions you have, or of all the things that are not clear to you about this play. Put each question on a separate piece of paper, fold it, and drop it into a box or bag. Pass the container around your group, each of you taking out one folded question. Give yourselves a time-limit, and then answer the question you picked as best you can.

You might ask the person who wrote the question to comment on the effectiveness of your answer.

5. You have been asked to organize a modern masque for a wedding. Before you make your plans, do the following:
   • Do some research to find out what masques were and what activities they included.
   • Decide what type of masque would be appropriate for a wedding celebration.
   • Decide on details of the masque, such as music, characters, story-line and costumes.
   • Plan what form of presentation you will use. You might consider preparing a report, using a scrapbook format (with drawings, notes, and illustrations from magazines) or you might choose to perform the masque on a "Drama Day."

6. In Act One, Scene One, Hermia says "O hell! to choose love by another's eyes " (line 140). A few lines later (line 234), Helena says "Love looks not with the eyes, but with the mind." These lines include two of the many statements made in this play about love and seeing, or love and understanding.

Review the play, writing down as many of these statements as you can find. When you are finished, decide if you can find any pattern in the statements. Consider the personality of the character making the statement and the place where the character makes the statement, i.e., the city or the forest.

Write an article for a psychology magazine expressing your opinion about the connection between love and seeing and love and understanding.

7. As you were reading through the play, you probably observed that characters used different styles of speech for different occasions. Some speeches appear in rhymed poetry, some appear in unrhymed poetry (blank verse), and some appear in prose.

   Find one or two examples of each style of speech in the play. Practise saying the speech aloud in one of the two other styles. What did you discover? Present your findings to your group.

8. As a set designer, you are having a problem designing a set for the forest that creates the impression of the forest being both "enchanted" and a real one that human characters visit.

   How would you create the combination of real with unreal in a forest set design?

   Write a description of your forest and the impression you want it to give the audience. You could develop an illustration of your forest design to accompany your written account.

9. As Theseus, you want the three-wedding event to be one your guests will never forget. You decide to prepare a public announcement of the event that describes the planned festivities.

   Write the announcement, detailing the wedding-day events that you will read to the citizens of Athens.

10. As Queen Elizabeth I, you have just returned to your palace after seeing Shakespeare's latest work, *A Midsummer Night's Dream*. You think that Shakespeare developed the character of Titania using some of your characteristics as his model.

Do you feel flattered or upset by the parallel he draws between the two of you?

Write a letter to Shakespeare explaining how you feel about Titania and whether you think there are any similarities between you and this Queen of the Forest.

11. Puck refers to himself and the other characters of the forest as being "shadows."

Why do you think he uses the word "shadow" to describe himself? From your own point of view, explain whether the word "shadows" is an appropriate word to describe the forest people. Find other dictionary meanings for *shadow* that Puck might be hinting at. In your journal, indicate whether you think these meanings do or do not apply to the forest people.

12. A government official in London, England, during the sixteen hundreds whose name was Samuel Pepys said after he saw the play, that it was the most dull and ridiculous play that Shakespeare ever wrote. Pepys became famous for his diary, which included his personal comments about social customs of the time.

Write a diary entry about *your* response to *A Midsummer Night's Dream*. Do you agree or disagree with Pepys? Explain your response.

13. As Oberon, you have the ability to cast spells on others. Decide who you would like to have under your spell, and what kind of spell you would want to cast on the person. In your journal, compose a poetic form of your spell. Write a description of the situation you would create for casting your spell and what would happen when the spell takes place.

14. Shakespeare floods his play with moonlight and with references to the moon. The only time action occurs in daylight is during the first part of Act 4, Scene 1.

In Act 3, Scene 1, Bottom has Quince check the almanac to see if the moon will actually shine on the night of their performance, since Pyramus and Thisbe are to meet by moonlight. Look through the play to find other references made to the moon.

Find out some of the beliefs people have had about the moon. Contrast these beliefs about the moon with scientific information we have today.

Why was it appropriate for Shakespeare to "flood" this play in moonlight?

15. There are three kinds of love revealed in this play, the love of the young people (Hermia, Lysander, Helena and Demetrius), the love of the older people (Theseus and Hippolyta), and the love of the forest people (Oberon and Titania).

    In your opinion, what characteristics and qualities do each of the three sets of lovers demonstrate?

    Write a description of the kind of love they show for one another.

    As you prepare your response, consider the following questions:
    • How did they gain the love of each other?
    • How did they (or would they) respond to a threat to the love relationship?
    • What kind of lifetime love partnership would they have?

    After you have completed your descriptions, decide what you think Shakespeare is saying about love and discuss your ideas with your group.

16. Have members of different groups select two or three lines from major speeches in the play and write them on pieces of paper.

    Fold the papers, assign names or numbers to the different groups, and write the appropriate name or number on the outside.

Drop the papers into a bag and give the bag to your teacher.

Have your teacher select two groups to be the first contestants. Each group should select speech lines from the bag that were not written by either goup.

The group that can successfully identify the speaker of the lines continues to play against other groups.

At the end of the game, have a discussion among your groups about which speech you think is the best one in the play. Give your reasons for your choice.